RUSTICA

RUSTICA

DELICIOUS RECIPES FOR VILLAGE-STYLE MEDITERRANEAN FOOD

THEO A. MICHAELS

PHOTOGRAPHY BY MOWIE KAY

rps

RYLAND PETERS & SMALL
LONDON • NEW YORK

Dedication

For my family and the generations before us.

Art director
Leslie Harrington

Senior designer
Sonya Nathoo

Editorial director
Julia Charles

Head of production
Patricia Harrington

Publisher
Cindy Richards

Food stylist
Kathy Kordalis

Prop stylist
Olivia Wardle

Indexer
Hilary Bird

First published in 2020 by
Ryland Peters & Small
20–21 Jockey's Fields
London WC1R 4BW
and
341 E 116th St
New York NY 10029

www.rylandpeters.com

10 9 8 7 6 5 4 3 2 1

Text © Theo A. Michaels 2020
Design and photographs
© Ryland Peters & Small 2020

ISBN: 978-1-78879-280-6

Printed in Slovenia

A CIP record for this book is available from the British Library. US Library of Congress Cataloging-in-Publication Data has been applied for.

IMPORTANT NOTES FOR COOKS

• OVENS: The recipes in this book have been tested in a fan oven.
• MEASURES: Both British (Metric) and American (Imperial plus US cups) are included within these recipes for your convenience, however, it is important to work with one set of measurements only when cooking.
• HERBS: All herbs used are fresh unless specified as dried.
• CITRUS ZEST: When a recipe calls for the grated zest of citrus fruit, buy unwaxed fruit and wash well before using. If you can only find treated fruit, scrub well in warm, soapy water before using.

• OLIVE OIL: Extra-virgin olive oil is the highest quality oil. It is unrefined, contains antioxidants and anti-inflammatories and has a low smoke point and heightened flavour. It is best saved for dressings. Refined olive oil is milder in flavour and contains less health benefits but its higher smoke point makes it more suitable for cooking.
• BEANS: Precooked canned beans are used in these recipes for convenience. If however you would prefer to use dried beans, convert them as follows, then soak and cook as appropriate to the variety before using as instructed:
  400-g/14-oz. can cooked beans once drained yields 250 g/1 cup
  115-g/heaping ½ cup dried beans once cooked yields 250 g/1 cup (equivalent to 1 can of cooked)
• STERILIZING JARS: Sterilize glass jars for use before filling with preserves. Preheat the oven to 150°C fan/160°C/325°F/Gas 3. Wash the jars and lids in very hot soapy water and rinse but don't dry them. Remove any rubber seals, put the jars onto a baking sheet and into the oven for 10 minutes. Soak the lids in boiling water for a few minutes before using.

CONTENTS

INTRODUCTION

Rustica [ruhs-ti-kah]
Definition:
adj. humble; rural; frugal; peasant food; honest
n. cookbook celebrating the simple beauty of uncomplicated
village food from the Mediterranean

What follows is a collection of over 65 recipes inspired by Mediterranean village life; pages filled with simple yet delicious food, based on traditional dishes cooked across the region, but developed with modern life in mind. Some recipes are classics, while others are my fresh twists on traditional techniques and ingredients. My aim is to share my enthusiasm for this style of food and cooking with you, and also to offer you a blueprint for a simpler, more balanced way of eating. My recipes are not contrived or designed to be 'healthy'. I just want to encourage you to eat in a naturally balanced way by enjoying good quality seasonal ingredients, sensible portion sizes, a few treats and a tumbler or two of wine – simple, frugal, humble eating.

My own family hail from Cyprus, coming originally from villages dotted all over the island. It is through conversations with them over the years that I have been able to paint a picture of what life might have been like a generation or two back, and this has shaped my 'village food' philosophy. They typically grew their own produce, foraged and fished, and also kept some small livestock, such as chickens, pigs, goats and rabbits, which gave them meat plus eggs, milk, butter and the means to make cheeses. Sourcing food this way automatically meant eating in tune with the seasons and a higher intake of vegetables, fruit, pulses, grains and nuts. Meat and fish, often considered a luxury, were reserved for feast days and celebrations. What was in effect a 'Mediterranean diet' (now recognized as one of the healthiest in the world) came from a place of necessity in these rural communities.

What I love in particular about this Mediterranean style of cooking is the alchemy of simple, often frugal ingredients morphing into something delicious. It was built on the foundations of 'low-waste kitchens' and 'nose-to-tail eating', long before these phrases were coined. Never has stale bread tasted so good as when it is transformed into Pangritata, breadcrumbs fried until crisp in olive oil with garlic, and used in place of Parmesan (see page 130) or foraged wild greens and dandelions, pulled from the earth to be laced until silky with olive oil and become Garlic Horta (see page 122). When an animal is killed it is old and every part is used. A hen, tough as old boots, long retired from her egg-laying career, is used to make a flavoursome soup (see Avgolemono on page 108) or a frugal cut of meat will be slow-cooked in wine with herbs until it melts into something delicious, like my Oxtail Osso Buco on page 118. We should all also consider broadening our horizons and embrace meats like farmed rabbit (see Rabbit Pepitoria on page 117) and even goat; both sustainable choices.

My recipes feature all the headline acts you'd expect to find; olives and oregano from Greece, pasta and tomatoes from Italy, almonds and saffron from Spain and lentils and potatoes from France. I celebrate the food eaten in all these countries, and the ingenious and diverse ways that they use these ingredients, which are common to all of them.

Rustica is a cookbook, yes, but do consider it a starting point. Sure, you can run with me and cook my recipes just as I do, but feel free to add a little of this and leave out a little of that. I use drizzles and splashes, a pinch of this and a handful of that and I want you to feel comfortable doing the same, don't overthink it, have fun. Ultimately, it's these nuances and the personality of a cook that are the most important ingredient.

Theo x

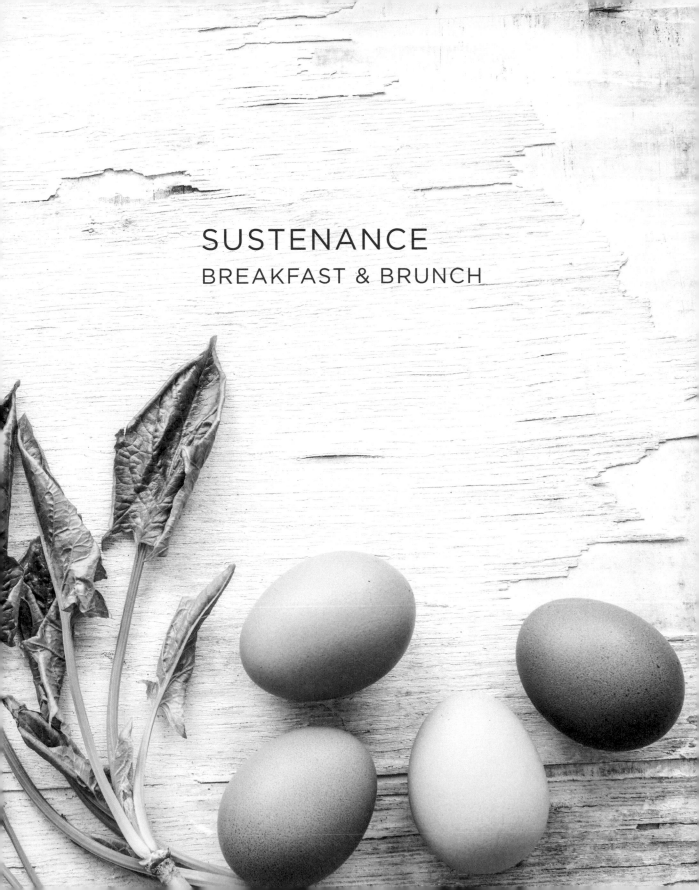

SUSTENANCE
BREAKFAST & BRUNCH

SOCCA WITH CHARRED ASPARAGUS & SPICED LABNEH

Socca are delicious savoury pancakes that originate from Nice in France and make a delicious breakfast or brunch. They are simple to make, the main ingredients being gram (chickpea) flour and water, making these both vegan and gluten free. They are not as pliable as conventional pancakes, so better topped rather than filled and rolled up, and here charred asparagus and my Spiced Labneh do the job nicely (see recipe on page 127).

12 fresh asparagus spears
butter, for frying/sautéing
a pinch of chilli/hot red pepper
    flakes
a pinch of toasted cumin seeds
runny honey, to drizzle
leaves from a few sprigs of
    coriander/cilantro
lemon wedges, for squeezing
salt and freshly ground black
    pepper, to season
1 quantity Spiced Labneh,
    to serve (see page 127)

For the Socca Pancakes
100 g/¾ cup gram (chickpea)
    flour
½ teaspoon baking powder
a pinch of salt
leaves picked from 1 thyme sprig,
    or ½ teaspoon dried thyme
1 tablespoon olive oil, plus a
    splash for frying/sautéing

Serves 4

First make the pancake batter. Combine the gram flour, baking powder, salt, thyme and 1 tablespoon of olive oil in a bowl with 225 ml/1 scant cup cold water and whisk until smooth; you are aiming for a single/light cream consistency. Leave the batter to rest for a minimum of 10 minutes at room temperature (or even overnight in the fridge, to give the gram flour time to fully absorb the liquid).

Trim the woody ends off the asparagus spears at an angle. Heat a frying pan/skillet set over a high heat and drop the spears into the hot pan, along with a small knob/pat of butter. Season generously with salt, pepper and a pinch of chilli/hot red pepper flakes. Fry/sauté for a couple of minutes over a high heat and then remove from the pan whilst still firm. Place, uncovered, in a low oven to keep warm until ready to serve.

Using the same frying pan/skillet, heat a splash of olive oil and once shimmering pour in about half a ladleful of the batter to make a thin 20-cm/8-inch pancake. Cook for a few minutes until the pancake sets and bubbles just start to appear on its surface. Flip it over before fully cooked and cook for a further 30 seconds, before removing from the pan. Repeat until you have at least 4 pancakes, keeping them warm on a plate and covered with foil.

To assemble the dish, put a pancake on a serving plate and smear a few spoonfuls of Spiced Labneh across the surface, top with the cooked asparagus spears, add a pinch of cumin seeds and a drizzle of honey, and garnish with a sprinkle of coriander/cilantro leaves. Serve with lemon wedges on the side for squeezing.

STRAPATSADA

Greek *strapatsada* is essentially a three-ingredient recipe; scrambled eggs with tomatoes and feta cheese. I find it a little sharp tasting and prefer a dish with more rounded flavours so add a few fresh herbs and spices and a little heat to mine to help kickstart the day. It's also really good served with some home-made croûtons to add a satisfying crunch. It is surprisingly filling so make this for brunch rather than breakfast and if you're feeling carnivorous throw in a few slices of cooked smoked sausage.

3 ripe tomatoes
2 tablespoons olive oil
½ green (bell) pepper, deseeded and sliced
3 spring onions/scallions, sliced
1 green jalapeño chilli/chile, sliced
½ garlic clove, crushed
¼ teaspoon ground cumin
¼ teaspoon paprika
½ tablespoon dried oregano
a pinch of sugar
80 g/3 oz. feta cheese, broken into large chunks
3 eggs, whisked
a handful of mixed green herbs, such as flat-leaf parsley, coriander/cilantro, dill and mint, roughly torn
¼ red onion, very thinly sliced
salt and freshly ground black pepper, to season

For the croûtons
1 slice rustic bread, cut into 1.5-cm/½-inch cubes
2 tablespoons olive oil

Serves 4

Preheat the oven to 200°C fan/220°C/425°F/Gas 7.

To make the croûtons, put the cubed bread in a bowl, season with salt and pepper and toss with the olive oil. Tip onto a baking sheet and bake in the preheated oven for 4 minutes, until golden and crisp. Remove and let cool.

Deseed the tomatoes and chop the flesh. Put the flesh in a sieve/strainer set over a bowl and let the juices run out.

Meanwhile, put the olive oil in a saucepan and set over a medium heat. Add the green (bell) pepper and spring onions/scallions and fry/sauté for 2 minutes, then add the chilli/chile, garlic, cumin, paprika and oregano. After a further 2 minutes, add the drained tomatoes to the pan along with the sugar. Season with salt and pepper and simmer until the tomatoes have broken down, adding a splash of water if they start to dry out. When they are completely soft, turn down the heat and fold in half the feta cheese chunks and most of the fresh herbs, reserving some to garnish.

Using the back of a spoon, make a few indents in the tomato sauce around the edge of the pan and pour in the eggs. Now, still using the back of a spoon, drag a line from the eggs through the tomato mixture which will fill up with the runny egg. Do this several times, gently and slowly, until the egg is just about set then remove the pan from the heat and let it rest for a few minutes.

To serve, gently slide your strapatsada onto a serving plate, scatter over the remaining feta cheese chunks, thinly sliced red onion and reserved herbs and scatter over the croûtons.

SMOKED HADDOCK & EGGS 'EN COCOTTES'

These French-inspired baked eggs wallow in a creamy sauce made from a smoked haddock poaching liquor and cheese and are just begging to be served with crisp toast for dipping. A little shredded cavolo nero or chard adds just a touch of bitterness, but fresh spinach does the job too. This recipe makes one 2-egg cocotte to share or split the recipe and make individual ones if you want one all to yourself.

a handful of cavolo nero (Italian black cabbage) or fresh spinach/chard, shredded
2 tablespoons olive oil
150 ml/⅔ cup whole milk
1 dried bay leaf
6 cloves
100 g/3½ oz. undyed smoked haddock fillet, skin-on
1 tablespoon plain/all-purpose flour
30 g/¼ cup grated Comté or Gruyère cheese, or similar
2 small eggs
chopped flat-leaf parsley leaves, to garnish
salt and freshly ground black pepper, to season
toasted rustic bread, to serve

a 10-cm/4-inch ramekin or 2 small individual ones, as preferred

a roasting pan, large enough to hold the ramekin(s)

Serves 2

Preheat the oven to 180°C fan/200°C/400°F/Gas 6.

Add the cavolo nero and 1 tablespoon of the olive oil to a frying pan/skillet and fry/sauté for a few minutes. Add a few drops of water and let it steam. Cook until the pan is dry, then tip the cavolo nero into the bottom of the ramekin(s) and spread it out into an even layer.

Pour the milk into a medium saucepan and add the bay leaf and cloves. Bring the milk to a simmer over a low heat and add the haddock fillet, skin-side down. Poach for 6–8 minutes depending on the thickness of the fillet. Remove the haddock from the poaching liquor using a slotted spoon and, when cool enough to handle, use a fork to flake the flesh into the ramekin(s) to join the cavolo nero.

Combine the remaining 1 tablespoon of olive oil with the flour in a small dish and mix until fully incorporated. Pass the poaching liquor through a sieve/strainer and return it to the poaching pan. Set the pan over a low heat and add the flour and olive oil paste. Heat to a simmer, whisking continuously, until the mixture starts to thicken. Remove the pan from the heat and stir in half the grated cheese until melted and incorporated into the sauce. Season generously with salt and pepper.

Pour the sauce over the haddock in the ramekin(s). Make a couple of small wells in the sauce, crack an egg into each one, letting a little of the white fall away first before pouring in the rest of the egg. Sprinkle the remaining grated cheese over the top and place the dish in a roasting pan filled with enough just-boiled water to come about halfway up the sides of the ramekin(s).

Carefully transfer the pan to the preheated oven and bake the cocotte(s) for about 10 minutes for a slightly runny egg. Garnish with a sprinkle of flat-leaf parsley and serve with toast for dipping.

MEDITERRANEAN ROSTI
WITH GREEN TOMATO SOFRITO

These fresh and sharp-tasting courgette/zucchini, potato and feta rosti
are fried until crisp and then topped with an egg and a tangy green tomato
sofrito sauce. My advice is make more sofrito than you think you need; it is
very moreish and I always wish I had another spoonful when I run out...

100 g/3½ oz. floury potatoes,
   unpeeled but well scrubbed
50 g/2 oz. courgette/zucchini
40 g/1½ oz. medium red or
   white onion, thinly sliced
40 g/1½ oz. feta cheese,
   crumbled
a generous pinch of dried mint
   or leaves from 3 sprigs of mint,
   finely chopped
2 tablespoons olive oil
2 eggs, for poaching
a splash of white wine vinegar,
   for poaching the eggs
salt and freshly ground black
   pepper, to season

For the Green Tomato Sofrito
about 2 tablespoons olive oil
1 red onion, finely diced
½ green (bell) pepper, deseeded
   and finely diced
1 garlic clove, crushed
1 fresh green chilli/chile, diced
3 large green tomatoes,
   deseeded and flesh chopped
6 sprigs of flat-leaf parsley,
   chopped
6 sprigs of coriander/cilantro,
   chopped
salt and freshly ground black
   pepper, to season

Serves 2

To make the Green Tomato Sofrito, add a splash of olive oil to a large frying pan/skillet and add the onion, (bell) pepper, garlic and chilli/chile. Fry/sauté very gently over a low heat for about 10 minutes, until softened and starting to caramelize. Season with salt and pepper.

Add the green tomatoes, flat-leaf parsley and coriander/cilantro (including the stalks) and simmer for another 20 minutes over a low heat, or until the sauce has thickened – add a splash of water if it starts to catch. Once cooked, fold in a little more olive oil to give it a silky finish, cover and set aside until ready to use.

Grate the potatoes (on the side of your box grater with the largest holes), then use your hands to squeeze out the excess liquid from the potatoes. Put in a mixing bowl. Grate the courgette/zucchini in the same way and again squeeze the excess liquid out. Add to the bowl with the grated potato. Fold in the sliced onion, feta cheese and mint. This should be quite a dry mixture.

Heat the olive oil in a non-stick frying pan/skillet set over a high heat. Grab a quarter of the rosti mixture and use your hands to form it into a tight ball, then flatten to about 2 cm/¾ inch thick and put into the hot oil. Repeat to make 4 rostis. The secret to success here is not to touch the rostis while they are cooking as you need a strong crust to form and hold it all together. After about 5 minutes use a fish slice to gently flip them over and cook for a further 5 minutes, again without disturbing them. Remove the rostis from the pan and keep warm in a low oven until ready to serve.

To poach the eggs, bring a small saucepan of water to a simmer with a drop of vinegar, swirl the water then slide an egg out of its shell and into the centre, poach for about 4 minutes until the white is cooked, then carefully remove with a slotted spoon and drain on paper towels. Repeat with the second egg.

Divide the rostis between serving plates, add an egg, spoon the Green Tomato Sofrito generously over the top and serve.

MICHAELS' MORNING TORTILLA DE PATATAS WITH FRESH TOMATO SALSA

The combination of eggs, potatoes and onions creates something that is more than the sum of its parts. Inspired by the eggs my dad used to hash together for us as kids, my tortilla-making technique might be traditional but the addition of other ingredients isn't, and it's the way I like it because it reminds me of those family breakfasts. Whatever you do, don't overcook it, you want a slight wobble.

250 ml/1 cup olive oil
1 medium white or red onion, sliced
350 g/¾ lb. waxy potatoes, peeled, halved and sliced
5 eggs
60 g/⅔ cup grated strong/sharp Cheddar cheese
80 g/½ cup smoked bacon lardons/cubed thick-cut smoked bacon
¼ green (bell) pepper, deseeded and diced
salt and freshly ground black pepper, to season

For the Fresh Tomato Salsa
150 g/5½ oz. baby plum tomatoes, diced
1 tablespoon finely diced red onion
½ fresh green chilli/chile, deseeded and diced
2 tablespoons chopped flat-leaf parsley
3 tablespoons olive oil
1 tablespoon cider vinegar
salt and freshly ground black pepper, to season

a 20-cm/8-inch non-stick, deep frying pan/skillet

Serves 4

To make the Fresh Tomato Salsa, combine all the ingredients in a small bowl, season generously with salt and pepper, cover and set aside.

Add the oil and onion to a frying pan/skillet set over a medium heat and fry/sauté for about 6–8 minutes, or until the onion starts to caramelize, then add the potatoes and continue cooking for about 10–15 minutes more, until the potatoes soften.

Meanwhile, crack the eggs into a mixing bowl, season generously with salt and pepper and break them up with a fork (there is no need to whisk them), then tip in the grated cheese.

Use a slotted spoon to remove the cooked onion and potatoes from the pan (leaving the oil behind) and fold them into the egg mixture. Cover the bowl and let the mixture steep for 15 minutes, after which time the mixture will have thickened as the potatoes soak up moisture from the eggs.

Put the pan back over the heat and fry/sauté the lardons for a few minutes before adding the (bell) pepper. When the lardons have turned golden, add them and the pepper to the bowl with the eggs. Wipe the pan with paper towels, leaving a little residual oil.

Heat up the pan again and once it's hot, pour in the egg mixture – it will fill most of the pan. Cook over a medium-high heat for about 4–5 minutes, until the tortilla is just pulling away from the edge of the pan, it will still be runny in the centre. Lay a plate larger than the pan over the tortilla, hold it firmly, then confidently flip it over so the tortilla is now resting on the plate and the pan is upside-down on top.

Put the pan back on the heat and gently slide the tortilla off the plate and back into the pan. Continue cooking for just a couple of minutes, then place a clean plate back on top of the pan again and flip it out. Leave to rest for a few minutes before serving.

Sieve/strain the Fresh Tomato Salsa and discard the excess liquid. Spoon it in a little pile in the centre of your tortilla and serve.

HELLENIC BREAKFAST BOARD

One of my most vivid memories of visiting relatives in Cyprus as a child was having breakfast at my great aunt's house. It was unlike anything I'd ever eaten before; not because of some incredible gastronomic alchemy, but because it was the definition of simplicity. It was exquisite, refreshing and I could feel my body thanking me for it. What's included on a breakfast board isn't set in stone… Sometimes a local sausage like spicy *pastirma* or red-wine-marinated *loukaniko* is a good addition, so you could add a good quality chorizo if you fancy it. I even remember having cold leftover poached chicken one morning; just tearing pieces off and dipping them into salt.

a 250-g/9-oz. halloumi cheese
4 eggs
340 g/1½ cups Greek yogurt
60 ml/4 tablespoons runny
    honey (preferably Greek)
a handful of pistachios or walnuts
400 g/14 oz. ripe vine tomatoes
5 ripe figs or watermelon slices
100 g/1 cup Kalamata olives
a large handful of rocket/arugula
extra virgin olive oil, to dress
salt and freshly ground black
    pepper, to season
a loaf of rustic bread, to serve

For the Marinated Feta
a 200-g/7-oz. feta cheese
1 garlic clove, unpeeled and
    cracked
1 tablespoon Greek dried
    oregano
1 dried red chilli/chile pepper
a few sprigs of fresh thyme
a few strips of lemon zest
freshly ground black pepper
80 ml/scant ⅓ cup extra virgin
    olive oil

*a large sealable glass jar,
    sterilized (for the feta)*

Serves 4–6

Marinated Feta: Drain and rinse the feta cheese and pat dry with paper towels. Either leave the feta whole, or break it into large chunks (about 6 cm/2 inches works well) and put them in your jar. Follow with the other ingredients, pouring in the oil last. Leave in the fridge for a few days before eating. (I like to put it on the board in the jar to serve.)

Halloumi: If it's good quality halloumi, you don't need to griddle it; it should be firm but soft enough to eat with a salty creaminess already laced with dried mint. Just cut a few slices to get things going and serve with a knife alongside.

Boiled/hard-cooked eggs: Pop the eggs into a saucepan of cold water, set over a medium heat and bring to the boil. Once the water is boiling, leave the eggs in for 6 minutes. Remove, rinse under cold water, shell and then rinse again and either leave whole or cut in half before dotting around the board.

Greek yogurt: Pour the yogurt into a shallow bowl, drizzle over the honey (Greek pine honey really is delicious so worth seeking some out), break up some of the nuts by giving them a little whack with the end of a rolling pin and scatter over the top.

Tomatoes: These had better be juicy, ripe and full-flavoured; cut a couple of them into wedges, season with a grinding of black pepper and a pinch of salt and group them together on the board. I tend to dip them in olive oil before eating, or you can dress them in a bowl.

To finish, dot halved figs or watermelon slices, Kalamata olives and rocket/arugula in small clusters around the board. Cut a few slices of bread, leaving the rest within reach with a knife. I like to smear some really good butter directly onto the board near the bread and add a little dish of olive oil nearby in case of an emergency…

CYPRIOT 'FUL MEDAMES'
WITH PRESERVED LEMON SALSA

Beans make up a substantial part of a village diet in the Mediterranean, as they are cheap, often locally grown and filling. This dish of spiced, crushed beans takes its inspiration from the Egyptian dish *Ful Medames*. Egypt is just visible from the island of Cyprus... so I've given it a Cypriot twist with cooling Greek yogurt and a sour-sweet preserved lemon salsa.

½ tablespoon cumin seeds
a splash of olive oil
1 red onion, diced
1 garlic clove, crushed
¼ teaspoon cayenne pepper
a cinnamon stick
1 large ripe tomato, diced
400-g/14-oz. can borlotti beans, drained and rinsed
160 ml/⅔ cup vegetable stock
a pinch of sugar
dried chilli/hot red pepper flakes, to garnish (optional)
a few coriander/cilantro leaves, to garnish
extra virgin olive oil, to dress
a few pinches of toasted sesame seeds
salt and freshly ground black pepper, to season
Greek yogurt and warmed pita breads, to serve

For the Preserved Lemon Salsa
1 tomato, deseeded and diced
1 tablespoon diced red onion
½ a preserved lemon, diced
2 tablespoons extra virgin olive oil
1 tablespoon white wine vinegar
1 tablespoon chopped coriander/cilantro

Serves 2

To make the Preserved Lemon Salsa, mix all the ingredients together in a small bowl and season with salt. Taste and add more extra virgin olive oil, vinegar or salt to taste. Set aside.

Toast the cumin seeds in a small, dry frying pan/skillet until just fragrant and tip into a mortar with ½ teaspoon of salt. Coarsely grind with a pestle and set aside.

Add a splash of olive oil to a large saucepan and fry/sauté the diced red onion for a few minutes, until it has softened and started to caramelize. Add the garlic, ground cumin seeds, cayenne pepper and cinnamon stick. Before the spices start to catch, add the tomato and let simmer for 1 minute. Season generously with salt and pepper.

Add the borlotti beans, hot stock and sugar to the pan. Leave uncovered over low heat and on a gentle simmer for about 5 minutes, until the liquid has reduced by half. Remove from the heat, discard the cinnamon stick and mash about half of the beans with a fork to get the mixture as smooth as possible – it will be a bit lumpy but you want texture so that's okay, just add a small splash of water if it's too thick.

Assemble the dish by spreading the warm bean mixture out on a serving plates and add a couple of tablespoonfuls of the Preserved Lemon Salsa. Finish with a drizzle of extra virgin olive oil, a sprinkle of toasted sesame seeds, a pinch of dried chilli/hot red pepper flakes (if using) and some torn coriander/cilantro leaves.

Serve with dollops of Greek yogurt and warmed pita breads.

RICOTTA PANCAKES
WITH CHERRY COMPOTE

These ricotta pancakes are light yet creamy at the same time and make for a decidedly luxurious brunch, especially when served with a deep purple cherry compote that contrasts in both flavour and colour. A glass of bubbly would not be inappropriate here and is, in fact, actively encouraged!

200 g/scant 1 cup ricotta cheese
200 ml/¾ cup whole milk
2 eggs, separated
1 teaspoon freshly squeezed
    lemon juice
140 g/1 generous cup plain/
    all-purpose flour
½ tablespoon baking powder
1 tablespoon caster/granulated
    sugar
butter, for shallow frying

For the Cherry Compote
400 g/14 oz. fresh cherries,
    destalked
30 g/2½ tablespoons caster/
    superfine sugar
a squeeze of fresh lemon juice

Serves 4

To make the cherry compote, stone/pit each cherry by squashing it with the flat side of a knife until you hit the stone/pit then rip open the cherry, remove the stone/pit and chuck the cherry flesh straight into a saucepan as you go. Add the sugar, lemon juice and 2 tablespoons of cold water to the pan. Bring to a boil over a medium heat, then reduce to a simmer and cook for 10–15 minutes, until the liquid thickens and the cherries are soft, adding more water if it starts to catch during cooking. Spoon into a bowl, cover and set aside.

Put the ricotta, milk, egg yolks and lemon juice in a large bowl and mix until well combined. Combine the flour, baking powder and sugar and then fold into the ricotta mixture. Finally, loosen the egg whites with a fork, no need to whisk them, and fold into the ricotta mixture.

Heat a knob/pat of butter in a frying pan/skillet set over a medium heat. Once it has melted pour in about half a ladleful of batter; this will make 10-cm/4-inch diameter pancakes, about 10–12 of them. Leave to cook for a few minutes, until you see bubbles appearing on the surface. This is your signal to flip the pancake over. Use a fish slice to do this and cook for a 2–3 minutes more. Once cooked remove from the pan. Repeat until all the batter has been used, keeping the pancakes warm in a low oven or on a plate and covered with foil as you go.

Stack the pancakes on serving plates, spoon over some of the Cherry Compote and serve warm.

CHURROS WITH MOCHA DIP

A popular Spanish treat, *churros* are frequently eaten in the morning for breakfast which always seems a little bit naughty (but I'm okay with that), occasionally for lunch and only ever once in my life have I had them for dinner! Traditionally made with butter and eggs, my recipe is usefully vegan and dairy-free but still has the desired crisp golden exterior and fluffy centre. Served in a haze of cinnamon sugar and with my morning espresso whipped into a chocolate dip on the side, I call this the perfect start to any day.

1 tablespoon ground cinnamon

2 tablespoons caster/superfine sugar, plus an extra pinch, divided

140 g/1 generous cup plain/ all-purpose flour

1 teaspoon baking powder

60 ml/¼ cup olive oil

vegetable oil, for deep frying

For the Mocha Dip

60 ml/¼ cup almond milk

90 g/3 oz. vegan dark/ bittersweet chocolate (minimum 70% cocoa), broken into pieces

30 ml/2 tablespoons freshly made espresso coffee, cooled

a piping/pastry bag fitted with a 2-cm/¾-inch star nozzle/tip or a disposable piping bag (note that a disposable bag won't give you the signature grooved surface)

Serves 2–4

Mix the cinnamon and sugar together in a small bowl and set aside.

Combine the flour with the baking powder and add the extra pinch of sugar. Pour 250 ml/1 cup cold water into a saucepan and set over a medium heat. Add the olive oil, bring the mixture to the boil, then remove it from the heat. Immediately shoot in the flour mixture and beat with a wooden spoon until it comes together; stop as soon as it starts to hold together and don't overwork it. It will be a sticky, slightly messy looking dough – and that's exactly what you want.

Spoon the dough into the prepared piping/pastry bag and push it down into the bag to remove any air-filled gaps.

Pour the vegetable oil into a large, heavy-based saucepan and set over a medium heat. You are good to go when a small piece of bread dropped into the oil sizzles but takes 1 minute to turn golden.

Line a plate or tray with paper towels. Carefully pipe the churros dough directly into the hot oil. Traditionally churros are in straight logs about 12–15 cm/5–6 inches long. If using a nozzle, just snip the batter into lengths with scissors as you pipe; if using a disposable bag just pinch the end of it when you want to break the piping.

Deep fry for about 5 minutes, until crisp and just starting to turn golden (these churros will remain a little paler than regular ones). Use a slotted spoon to transfer the cooked churros onto the lined plate or tray. Once slightly cooled sprinkle over the cinnamon sugar.

To make the Mocha Dip, put the almond milk and chocolate in a bowl and microwave for 30 seconds, stir to combine and mix in the coffee. Alternatively, heat the milk over a medium heat in a small saucepan and once it starts to bubble drop in the chocolate and whisk together until the chocolate melts. Finish by adding the shot of coffee.

Serve the warm churros as soon as possible with the Mocha Dip on the side for dunking

COMMUNITY
SMALL PLATES TO SHARE

GRIDDLED HALLOUMI & PEACH BRUSCHETTA
WITH HUMMUS & MINT

Here are the headline flavours of a Mediterranean summer, all resting on a slice of toasted sourdough. Charred sweet peaches, salty halloumi cheese, earthy hummus and zingy fresh mint, best served as part of a mezze and eaten in the sunshine with a glass of chilled white wine.

a little olive oil, just for griddling
  the bread
6 thin slices of sourdough bread
1 tablespoon demerara/turbinado
  sugar
3 fresh, ripe peaches, stoned/
  pitted and cut into 6 wedges
a 250-g/9-oz. halloumi cheese,
  cut into 6 slices
a pinch of paprika
leaves from a few sprigs of mint,
  torn
1 tablespoon toasted pine nuts
salt and freshly ground black
  pepper, to season
extra virgin olive oil, to drizzle
  (optional)

For the Hummus
400-g/14-oz. can chickpeas,
  drained and rinsed
1 garlic clove, crushed
1 tablespoon tahini (sesame seed
  paste)
½ tablespoon freshly squeezed
  lemon juice
4 tablespoons extra virgin
  olive oil
salt and freshly ground black
  pepper, to season

Serves 6

To make the hummus, put the chickpeas, garlic, tahini, lemon juice, extra virgin olive oil, a decent pinch of salt and pepper and 2 tablespoons of cold water into the bowl of a food processor. Pulse until you have an almost smooth paste. Use a spatula to scrape the hummus into a bowl, cover and set aside. Alternatively, but for a chunkier texture, mash by hand with a fork.

Heat a griddle pan over high heat. Brush or wipe a little olive oil over the sourdough slices and place them in the pan. Cook them for 1 minute then turn over to just brown the both sides. Remove them from the pan and set aside.

Sprinkle the sugar over the peach segments and put them in the same griddle pan but having reduced the heat to medium. Cook them for 1–2 minutes on each side until slightly browned and caramelized, then remove them from the pan and set aside.

Increase the heat of the pan until it is almost smoking then add the halloumi slices and cook them for 1 minute on each side, just long enough to brown, then remove from the pan.

To assemble the bruschetta, lay a slice of warm halloumi on each slice of griddled sourdough, add a dollop of hummus, then top each one with 3 peach wedges. Finish with a few grinds of black pepper, a little salt, a pinch of paprika and scatter over some torn mint leaves and toasted pine nuts.

I usually give them an extra drizzle of extra virgin olive oil but that's just me... serve as soon as possible.

HOME-CURED DUCK 'PROSCIUTTO'
WITH ROCKET & ORANGE VINAIGRETTE

This is, of course, not really prosciutto... but it is home cured and makes a fabulous dish to share. It takes a good few days to cure and then needs another few days to rest, but it's a great way of preserving a duck breast to use over a couple of weeks. I tend to find once it starts to dry out too much to enjoy on its own, it works nicely diced and fried to add to pasta or in a stew. Serve with a side of rocket/arugula dressed with a simple orange vinaigrette and a few Parmesan shavings. Note that the curing time will need to increase, the larger the duck breast you are using.

250-g/9-oz. duck breast
2 tablespoons freshly squeezed orange juice, plus a little finely grated orange zest to garnish
4 tablespoons extra virgin olive oil
1 tablespoon cider vinegar
salt and freshly ground black pepper, to season
a few handfuls of rocket/arugula, to serve

For the curing salt mixture
400 g/2 cups coarse sea salt
50 g/½ cup demerara/turbinado sugar
1 tablespoon freshly ground black pepper
1 dried bay leaf, ground to a powder with a pestle and mortar

Makes 12 servings

Trim the duck breast of any trailing bits of fat and if it has a very thick layer of fat on top, lightly trim this as well. Use a sharp knife to score the breast skin in diagonal lines, being careful not to pierce the flesh.

To make the curing salt mixture, simply mix together the salt, sugar, black pepper and ground bay leaf in a small bowl.

Choose a dish of material resistant to salt (ceramic or glass is best) into which the duck breast will fit snugly. Scatter a third of the curing salt mixture in the bottom (or enough to create a complete layer), then lay the duck flesh-side down and cover with the remaining mixture. Add more salt if any of the duck is exposed, you need it to be fully encased. Cover the top of the dish with clingfilm/plastic wrap and refrigerate for 3 days.

After 3 days the duck will have shrunk a little and be much firmer. Rinse off the salt, pat it with kitchen towels until fully dry and then loosely wrap it in baking parchment (you don't want it to be airtight, it needs a little air to allow the moisture to escape). Return it to the fridge for a further 5 days before serving.

When you are ready to serve, make the dressing by whisking together the orange juice, olive oil and vinegar until emulsified and season with a pinch each of salt and pepper. Slice the duck very thinly, starting at the thinner end and cutting at an angle. Arrange the slices on a plate with a little rocket/arugula, dressed with the orange vinaigrette and a sprinkle of orange zest, if you like.

You can store any leftover duck for next time, unsliced, in the fridge in an airtight container so that it doesn't dry out.

SEVILLE LAMB RIBLETS

Lamb riblets are an underused part of the animal, which is a shame. Cooked until almost crisp, these bones are the mast to a sail of deliciously rich meat. I prepare mine with a Seville orange marmalade sauce that cuts through the richness, making a pile of them a delight to devour.

a 700-g/1½-lb. lamb rib (also known as belly lamb), bone-in, cut into riblets
2 tablespoons sherry vinegar
1 teaspoon cumin seeds
2 tablespoons olive oil
4 tablespoons Seville orange marmalade/preserve
2 tablespoons cider vinegar
2 tablespoons caster/granulated sugar
1 garlic clove, crushed
1 fresh red chilli/chile pepper, deseeded and finely chopped (optional)
salt and freshly ground black pepper, to season

To garnish
sea salt flakes
a few sprigs of thyme
finely grated orange zest

Serves 4

Put the riblets in a single layer in a non-reactive dish and pour over the sherry vinegar. Add the cumin seeds and season generously with salt and pepper, massaging everything together with your hands. Cover and marinate overnight in the fridge or just go straight for cooking if you can't wait!

Preheat the oven to 160°C fan/180°C/350°F/Gas 4.

Arrange the marinated riblets on a baking sheet with plenty of space between them, drizzle over the olive oil and bake, uncovered, in the preheated oven for 1½ hours, until they are crisp around the edges.

To make the sauce, combine the marmalade, cider vinegar, sugar, garlic and chilli/chile (if using) in a small saucepan and set over a medium heat. Bring to the boil and as soon as the mixture bubbles, reduce the heat to a simmer, cook for 2 further minutes, then remove from the heat.

Spoon half the sauce onto a serving dish or board, pile the ribs on top and drizzle over the remaining sauce. Add a sprinkling of sea salt flakes, scatter over the thyme sprigs and orange zest to garnish and serve with plenty of napkins for wiping sticky fingers and chins!

VEGETABLE ANTIPASTI PLATE

Preserving vegetables in oil is a long-established means of saving a glut of summer produce for scarcer months. These Italian-style mushrooms, aubergines/eggplant and tomatoes are delicious served as an antipasti plate with plenty of rustic bread for dipping in the seasoned oil. To make a more substantial grazing board you could add some good marinated olives, a few chunks of Parmesan, a fresh mozzarella or burrata cheese and/or slices of cured Italian meats. These vegetables also work brilliantly as an ingredient in a host of recipes, from salads to pasta dishes, or do as I do and just spoon them straight onto some bread rubbed with garlic to enjoy as a sneaky snack.

PRESERVED WILD MUSHROOMS IN OIL

These lightly pickled wild mushrooms are delicious. My mate Biagio
introduced me to these. His father is from Naples and would forage for
mushrooms in Italy (and then in the UK). He would preserve such a bounty
of them that they would eventually find their way into our work-day lunches
together. Although a well-kept family secret, I reckon my recipe isn't too far
off of his dad's... Extremely versatile, my guilty pleasure is piling them high
on a piece of toast slathered in homemade *labneh* (see my recipe for Spicy
Labneh on page 127). I use a variety of mushrooms: chestnut, chanterelle,
porcini, morel... anything will work, as long as they are fresh and firm, and if
you can't source wild mushrooms, use cultivated button mushrooms instead.

500 g/18 oz. mixed wild
   mushrooms, such as porcini,
   chanterelle, chestnut and
   morel
400 ml/scant 1¾ cups cider
   vinegar
1 tablespoon wholegrain mustard
3 dried bay leaves
½ tablespoon coarse sea salt
½ tablespoon white sugar
60 ml/¼ cup olive oil
60 ml/¼ cup vegetable oil

a baking sheet, lined with
   parchment paper

a 500-ml/2-cup capacity sealable
   jar, sterilized

Makes 8–10 servings

Preheat the oven to 120°C fan/140°C/275°F/Gas 1.

Clean all the mushrooms by wiping them with a soft cloth or paper
towels and rinse them briefly under warm running water (but don't
soak them). Cut the bottom off the stalks, halve any larger mushrooms
and keep the small ones whole.

Put the vinegar, mustard, bay leaves, salt and sugar in a large
saucepan. Add 400 ml/scant 1¾ cups of cold water and set the pan
over a medium heat. Bring the liquid to the boil and then drop in the
mushrooms. Simmer for about 12 minutes, agitating them a little by
poking with a wooden spoon as they cook.

Using a slotted spoon, scoop the mushrooms out of the cooking
liquid onto a clean tea towel/dish cloth (it's okay to leave some of the
mustard seeds behind) and gently pat dry. Spread them out on the
lined baking sheet and put in the preheated oven for 20 minutes, just
to help them dry out.

Pour both the oils into a sterilized jar and add the mushrooms.
Make sure they are submerged in oil (top up with more if any are are
not). Sealed, these will keep in the fridge for up to 2 weeks. Once
opened use within 2 days.

PRESERVED AUBERGINES IN OIL

I like to griddle my aubergines/eggplant to give them a slight smokiness
before preserving. I say preserving... at home we scoff these at a rate of knots!

2 aubergines/eggplant, cut into
　　2-cm/¾-inch rounds
50 g/¼ cup coarse sea salt
450 ml/scant 2 cups cider
　　vinegar
150 ml/⅔ cup olive oil
150 ml/⅔ cup sunflower oil
a pinch of Greek dried oregano
1 sprig of thyme
1 garlic clove, sliced
1 whole dried chilli/chile pepper

*a 750-ml/3-cup capacity sealable
　glass jar, sterilized*

Makes 8–10 servings

Preheat the oven to 120°C fan/140°C/275°F/Gas 1.

Set a colander over a bowl and add the sliced aubergines/eggplant
and sprinkle with salt. Place a weighted plate on top and leave for
2 hours. Once the time is up, you'll see a pool of brown liquid in the
bowl. Discard this, rinse the slices under cold running water and then
squeeze them dry with a clean tea towel/dish cloth.

Heat a griddle pan over a high heat until smoking hot, then cook
the slices for a few minutes on each side, until lightly charred.

Put the vinegar in a saucepan with 450 ml/scant 2 cups cold water
and bring to a boil. Once you've got a rolling boil going drop the
aubergine/eggplant slices in. Wait 2 minutes then drain, put them on
a baking sheet and pop them into the preheated oven for 15 minutes.

Combine the oils and remaining ingredients in the jar, give it a
gentle shake and add the aubergine/eggplant slices, ensuring they are
fully submerged in the oil. Store in the fridge and eat within 2 weeks.

OVEN-ROASTED TOMATOES IN OIL

Roasting tomatoes very slowly in oil preserves them, intensifies their flavour
and gives them a silky melt-in-the-mouth texture.

1 kg/2¼ lb. mixed tomatoes
3 garlic cloves
400 ml/scant 1¾ cups olive oil
a sprig of thyme
a generous pinch of brown sugar
a pinch of coarse sea salt
salt and freshly ground black
　　pepper, to season
light olive oil, to top up

*a 750-ml/3-cup capacity sealable
　glass jar, sterilized*

Makes 8–10 servings

Preheat the oven to 120°C fan/140°C/275°F/Gas 1.

Halve each tomato, cutting from the top down, going through the
stalk, squeeze gently to pop out the watery flesh and seeds; use a
spoon if you have trouble. Slice the garlic cloves in half lengthways.

Line up the tomatoes, cut-side up, in a snug-fitting deep-sided,
baking sheet. Pour over the olive oil, add the thyme sprig, scatter the
garlic slices over the top, sprinkle with the sugar and season
generously with salt and pepper.

Bake in the preheated oven for 4 hours. Once the tomatoes have
dried out a little and become wrinkled, transfer to the jar, topping up
with light olive oil. Store in the fridge and eat within 2 weeks.

STUFFED CABBAGE PARCELS

Lahanodolmades are soft and succulent and make a delicious alternative to stuffed vine leaves; a slow braise tenderizes the cabbage wrapper and melts the meat and rice stuffing together. They are traditionally served with a Greek *avgolemono* (a creamy egg and lemon sauce) so I make a simpler lemon sauce without the eggs to go with them here, but they can be enjoyed with just a squeeze of lemon juice. You can serve them Greek-style at room temperature but my preference by far is warm straight from the oven – just make more than you think you will need, they will disappear quickly...

1 large savoy or white cabbage
a few splashes of olive oil
200 g/7 oz. minced/ground pork
200 g/7 oz. minced/ground beef
1 medium white onion, diced
2 garlic cloves, crushed
6 sprigs each of mint, flat-leaf
    parsley and dill, chopped
50 g/scant ½ cup pine nuts
150 g/¾ cup short-grain rice,
    uncooked
3 tablespoons tomato purée/
    paste
a pinch of paprika
a pinch of cayenne pepper
a pinch of ground cinnamon
½ teaspoon salt
500 ml/2 cups chicken stock
flat-leaf parsley and grated
    lemon zest, to garnish
    (optional)

For the sauce (optional)
1 tablespoon cornflour/cornstarch
freshly squeezed juice of 1 lemon
pan juices from the cabbage
    parcels
a small pinch of sugar

Makes about 20

Preheat the oven to 180°C fan/200°C/350°F/Gas 6.

Peel about 20 of the largest leaves from the cabbage, cutting away the thickest part of the stalk. Fill a large heatproof bowl with boiling water and add a pinch of salt. Put the leaves in the water for a few minutes to blanche, then remove and lay on a plate. (You'll need to do this in batches, being careful not to rip them.) Peel off some of the smaller leaves and reserve these to use later. Slice the remaining cabbage, use to line the base of a roasting pan and add a splash of oil.

Put the minced/ground meats in a mixing bowl and add all the other ingredients except the stock. Mix to combine.

Lay a blanched cabbage leaf out on a surface in front of you, vein-side down with the stalk end facing you. Take a ping pong ball-sized piece of filling, use your hands to roll it into a sausage shape and place it in the centre of the leaf, horizontally and closer to the stalk end. Fold the bottom edge up just enough to cover the filling, then fold both sides towards the middle and turn upwards and over to seal it and form a parcel. Place the parcels seam-side down in the cabbage-lined roasting pan, repeat until all the filling and blanched leaves are used up. Drizzle over a little oil and pour over the stock.

Cover the rolls with the reserved small leaves and then with foil, and bake in the preheated oven for 1½ hours. Once cooked, remove the foil and leave to rest for 15 minutes before serving.

To make the lemon sauce, mix the cornflour/cornstarch with the lemon juice in a small bowl to make a slurry. Pass the pan juices from the cabbage rolls through a sieve/strainer into a saucepan set over a medium heat. Whisk in the slurry and sugar, and heat until the sauce thickens. To serve, spoon some sauce over the parcels and add a sprinkle of flat-leaf parsley and a few pinches of lemon zest.

CHORIZO & BUTTER BEANS
IN HONEYED CIDER SAUCE

These little bites of chorizo are incredibly additive. Sautéed until they release their smoky oil, glazed with a sticky cider reduction and paired with creamy butter/lima beans, this dish is perfect served with nothing but chunks of rustic bread to soak up the juices and a good Rioja to wash it all down. You need soft cooking chorizo here, as opposed to the firmer, drier cured sausage that is usually sliced thinly and eaten raw as tapas.

olive oil, for frying/sautéing
400 g/14 oz. soft cooking chorizo, sliced into chunks
1 small white onion, finely sliced
1 whole dried chilli/chile pepper (optional)
2 garlic cloves, thickly sliced
400 ml/1¾ cups dry cider/dry hard cider
1 dried bay leaf
200-g/7-oz. can butter/lima beans, drained and rinsed
1 teaspoon runny honey, or more to taste
salt and freshly ground black pepper, to season
freshly chopped flat-leaf parsley, to garnish
chunks of rustic bread, to serve

Serves 4

Heat a little olive oil in a deep-sided, non-stick frying pan/skillet and add the chorizo. Fry/sauté for about 5 minutes, until the skin is slightly crisp. Carefully pour away any excess oil from the pan and add the onions and chilli/chile (If using). Fry/sauté the onions until they wilt and soften, then stir in the garlic.

Pour in the cider, add the bay leaf, season with salt and pepper and scrape the bottom of the pan to incorporate any caramelized bits of onion into the sauce. Simmer until the liquid has reduced by a third, then add the butter/lima beans and honey and continue cooking until you have a rich, thick sauce. Remove from the heat, taste and add more honey or salt and pepper to taste.

Transfer the chorizo and butter beans to a serving dish, spoon over the sauce and finish with a sprinkle of flaf-leaf parsley. Serve with chunks of rustic bread for dunking.

BLACKENED MACKEREL
WITH CRUNCHY CABBAGE SLAW

Fresh mackerel is not only beautiful, with its shimmering striped skin in hues of silver and blue, but is also utterly delicious when treated the right way. Cooked over a ferocious heat, just long enough to char and crisp the skin and cook the flesh from the bottom up, it only needs a squeeze of lemon juice to complement its rich, fishy flavour. This recipe pairs it with a crunchy red and white cabbage slaw.

4 fresh mackerel fillets, pin bones removed (the fresher the better)
a splash of olive oil
salt and freshly ground black pepper, to season
lemon wedges, for squeezing
sea salt flakes, to garnish

For the Crunchy Cabbage Slaw
100 g/1²⁄₃ cups shredded white cabbage
100 g/1²⁄₃ cups shredded red cabbage
1 medium carrot, peeled and grated
a handful of baby spinach leaves, torn
a small handful of flat-leaf parsley leaves, torn
a small handful of coriander/cilantro leaves, torn
3 tablespoons extra virgin olive oil
2 tablespoons freshly squeezed lemon juice
1 tablespoon Dijon mustard
1 teaspoon white wine vinegar
1 garlic clove, crushed

Serves 2

To make the Crunchy Cabbage Slaw, combine the red and white cabbage, carrot, spinach, flat-leaf parsley and coriander/cilantro in a mixing bowl. Whisk together the olive oil, lemon juice, mustard, vinegar and garlic in a small bowl (or do as I do and put in all in a screw-top jar, seal and shake). Set both elements aside until ready to assemble the dish. Don't be tempted to dress the salad too soon.

Using a sharp knife, cut 5 slits into the skin side of each mackerel fillet, just enough to break the skin but not cut into the flesh. Rub each one with a little olive oil, then season generously with salt and pepper. Heat a frying pan/skillet until smoking hot and place the mackerel fillets skin-side down in it. Immediately hold the fillets down flat with a spatula or fish slice for just for a few seconds to stop them curling. Cook for about 3 minutes, until the flesh starts to turn opaque but just a little of it along the centre of each fillet remains raw. The fillets should easily lift up from the pan, check the skin is nicely charred, then using a fish slice, turn each one over and cook for just 20 seconds flesh-side before removing from the pan one at a time and transferring to a paper-towel lined plate.

When you are ready to serve, fold the dressing into the slaw and transfer it to a serving platter or board. Arrange the mackerel fillets skin-side up over the top of the slaw and give them a little squeeze of lemon juice and sprinkling of sea salt flakes.

CHICKEN LIVERS IN BALSAMIC BUTTER
WITH PAN-SEARED PLUMS

Chicken livers are a part of the bird that often goes to waste, so they cost very little to buy but although a frugal ingredient, they can be delicious when delicately cooked. Here I've sautéed them in a tangy balsamic butter and paired with slightly charred, sour-sweet ripe plums.

1 tablespoon raspberry vinegar
2 tablespoons olive oil, plus extra for coating
1 teaspoon caster/granulated sugar
2 ripe plums, each cut into 8 wedges
200 g/7 oz. chicken livers
1 tablespoon butter
½ tablespoon balsamic vinegar
a handful of lamb's lettuce/corn salad
extra virgin olive oil, for dressing
salt and freshly ground black pepper, to season
slices of toasted sourdough bread, to serve

Serves 4

Whisk together the raspberry vinegar and olive oil in a salad bowl, season with salt and pepper and set aside.

Lightly sprinkle the sugar over the cut edges of the plum wedges. Heat a dry, non-stick frying pan/skillet over a high heat until smoking hot. Add the plums and cook for about 30 seconds on each side, just enough to colour them, then transfer them to a bowl and set aside.

Rinse the chicken livers, cut away any sinew and pat them dry with paper towels. Coat in a little olive oil and season generously all over with salt and pepper. Reheat the frying pan/skillet until hot, add the livers and cook them for 1½ minutes on each side. Remove the pan from the heat, and immediately drop in the butter followed by the balsamic vinegar. Swirl the pan to emulsify the liquid, letting the residual heat reduce it slightly, then toss the livers over to coat them. Tip the chicken livers into the bowl with the plums along with any remaining glaze from the pan.

Toss the lamb's lettuce/corn salad in the bowl of raspberry vinaigrette, shaking off any excess and scatter a few sprigs on a serving plate. Drain off any excess sauce from the livers and plums and arrange them in between the dressed lamb's lettuce/corn salad. Serve with toasted slices of sourdough bread.

Note: if you can't source raspberry vinegar, crush a couple of fresh raspberries in 60 ml/¼ cup white wine vinegar and pass through a sieve/strainer. Discard the raspberries and use the liquid.

SALT COD FRITTERS
WITH CAPER TZATZIKI

Originally a means of preserving fresh fish for leaner times, salt cod remains popular because of its distinctive flavour and texture. It is traditionally eaten in Greece at Easter, deep fried and served with *skordalia*, a creamy potato and olive oil dip, infused with garlic. My recipe pays homage to this but I encapsulate all the flavours of the *skordalia* in melt-in-the mouth fritters.

250 g/9 oz. salt cod (dried weight), refrigerated in a ceramic or glass bowl full of water for 24 hours before use
170 g/6 oz. floury potatoes, peeled and halved
1 tablespoon extra virgin olive oil
3 garlic cloves, crushed
1 tablespoon finely chopped dill
1 tablespoon finely chopped flat-leaf parsley
finely grated zest of 1 lemon
100 g/¾ cup plain/all-purpose flour
200 g/4 cups fresh breadcrumbs (see page 130)
1 egg
vegetable oil, for shallow frying
salt and freshly ground black pepper, to season

For the Caper Tzatziki
250 g/1½ cups Greek yogurt
1 tablespoon capers in vinegar, drained, coarsely chopped
1 teaspoon of vinegar from the caper jar
1 tablespoon finely chopped mint
a pinch of cayenne pepper
freshly squeezed lemon juice, to taste

Serves 4

Check the desalted and rehydrated cod over for small bones and discard any you find. Put it in a large saucepan, add just enough cold water to cover and set over a medium heat. Bring it to a very gentle simmer and poach for a few minutes, then turn off the heat. Let steep for a few minutes more, then drain and pat dry with paper towels.

Add the potatoes to a saucepan of boiling, unsalted water and cook for about 15 minutes, until just tender. Drain and leave uncovered to steam dry. Once dry, tip into a bowl and coarsely mash with a fork. Fold in the olive oil, garlic, dill, parsley and lemon zest. Season generously with salt and pepper. Flake the salt cod into the potato mixture and fold it all together. Cover and chill until needed.

Line up 3 bowls on your kitchen work surface. Put the flour in the first, break the egg into the second and beat it well with a fork, and put the breadcrumbs in the third. Line a tray with parchment paper.

Remove the salt cod and potato mixture from the fridge. Take an egg-sized piece and roll it into a cigar shape about 5 cm/2 inches long and 2.5 cm/1 inch diameter. Roll it in the flour, then dip in the egg and finally into the breadcrumbs to coat and lay it on the tray (I like to keep one hand 'wet', one hand 'dry' whilst doing this). Continue until all the mixture has been used and you have about 8 fritters.

Pour sufficient vegetable oil into a large heavy-based saucepan to reach a depth of 2.5 cm/1 inch and set over a medium-high heat. It is ready when a piece of bread dropped in takes 30 seconds to turn golden. Line a plate with paper towels and set to one side. Carefully drop the fritters in the oil and fry them for 3 minutes, or until golden, then gently turn over and cook the other side for a further 2 minutes. Once golden, transfer to the lined plate to drain.

To make the Caper Tzatziki, combine the yogurt, capers, vinegar, mint and cayenne pepper. Add a squeeze of lemon juice and mix together. Serve the fritters hot with the Caper Tzatziki on the side.

HOME-CURED ANCHOVIES

Throughout the Mediterranean it is the cheap, small fish that form a major part of the staple diet. Abundant in local waters and full of healthy fats, *gavros* (the Greek name for anchovies) are delicious once cured and served with some really good bread and a glass of wine (or *ouzo* as the case may be!). If you can't find fresh anchovies, sprats work just as well and belong to the same family of fish, and that's what I use. I've used smoked sea salt to cure these, but regular coarse sea salt will work just as well but not give the fish a pleasing hint of smokiness.

12 fresh sprats
about 50 g/¼ cup coarse smoked
    sea salt or coarse sea salt
100 ml/generous ⅓ cup sherry
    vinegar
freshly squeezed juice of 1 lemon
a 5-cm/2-inch piece of lemon
    zest
1 garlic clove, thickly sliced
2 dried bay leaves
a pinch of Greek dried oregano
250 ml/1 cup light olive oil
a few pink peppercorns, crushed,
    to garnish (optional)
lemon wedges, for squeezing
chunks of rustic bread, to serve

*a 750-ml/3-cup capacity sealable
glass jar, sterilized*

Makes 8 servings

Fillet the sprats, discarding the head, bones and guts (or ask your fishmonger to do this for you when you buy them).

Scatter a quarter of the salt on a plate that won't react with the salt, so ceramic, glass, plastic or stainless steel. Layer the sprat fillets on top, salting between each layer. These don't need to be fully encased in salt so you should have enough but use a little more if you feel you need to. Cover and put them in the fridge for 6 hours.

Put the sherry vinegar and lemon juice in a small bowl and whisk to combine. Remove the sprats from the fridge, rinse the salt off them and pat them dry with paper towels. Put them in a shallow dish and pour over the sherry vinegar and lemon juice mixture. Shuffle them around to ensure they are all submerged, cover and let them pickle in the fridge for 1 hour. Remove them from the pickling liquor, shaking off some of the excess.

Add the lemon zest, garlic, bay leaves and oregano to your jar. Add the cured sprat fillets and pour in the olive oil to cover. These are best eaten after a day or two so that they have time to soak in the flavours but refrigerate them until ready to serve and eat them within 3 days.

To serve, lay your 'gavros' out flat on a plate, leave for 10 minutes to take the fridge chill off and drizzle with some of the oil from the jar (if the oil has solidified just leave 1–2 tablespoon of it to liquify at room temperature) and scatter over some crushed pink peppercorns (if using). Add a few lemon wedges for squeezing and serve with chunks of rustic bread and that glass of white wine I mentioned earlier...

DANDELION TEMPURA

I'm rather proud of this one. The unassuming dandelion, a weed as hardy as they come, is a surprising nutrient superhero, loaded with vitamins, minerals and fibre. Their bright yellow flowers pop up all around the world; as I write I look out into my Hertfordshire garden in England and can spot yellow pockets dotted all around. Every part of the dandelion is edible and they are commonly used in recipes throughout the Mediterranean, and in Greece in particular. Pick dandelions from your own garden or local park, give them a rinse under running water and shake dry before cooking. This way of cooking them in a light tempura batter creates a perfect balance between bitter and sweet, crispy and soft; they are a dream to eat and so readily available, literally food there for the taking! Try to find young dandelions where the stalks are still quite delicate.

12 fresh dandelion flowers,
   including stalks
12 fresh dandelion leaves
vegetable oil, for deep frying
30 g/2 tablespoons self-raising/
   rising flour
30 g/2 tablespoons cornflour/
   cornstarch
100 ml/generous ⅓ cup sparkling
   water/soda
icing/confectioners' sugar,
   to dust
salt

Serves 6

Fill a bowl with cold water, add the dandelion flowers and leaves and gently submerge them in it. Move them about gently to clean them, then remove them from the bowl, shake off the excess water and set them on a plate lined with paper towels to dry. (If it's nice day, I'll leave mine in the sunshine for 10 minutes to help dry them out.)

Pour sufficient oil into a large, heavy-based saucepan to reach a depth of 2.5 cm/1 inch and set over a medium heat.

While the oil is heating up, make the tempura batter. Combine the self-raising/rising flour and cornflour/cornstarch and a pinch of salt in a mixing bowl. Pour in the sparkling water/soda and lightly whisk with a fork but don't over whisk it – a few lumps in the batter is good.

Line a plate or tray with paper towels. Test the oil is hot enough by dropping a little batter into the oil; it should bubble immediately but not turn golden for 20 seconds.

Using tongs, lightly dip each flower and leaf in the tempura batter and drop them straight into the hot oil as you go, they will take 45 seconds to cook. Turn them once during that time and then remove them from the oil before they start to colour and place on the paper towel-lined plate/tray to drain. Repeat until all the flowers and leaves are cooked.

Serve spaced out on a dish rather than on top of each other, and finish with a very light dusting of icing/confectioners' sugar just before serving.

INSALATA DI MARE

This unbeatable Italian celebration of seafood and shellfish stems from coastal dwellers eating whatever was caught or pulled from the sea that day in its humblest form. You can recreate it by using whatever fresh seafood you can source. I like to serve mine with an uncomplicated dry, white wine served out of a chipped terracotta carafe, some chunks of rustic bread to dunk in the juices and a loud passionate Italian for company...

4 tablespoons olive oil
1 tablespoon freshly squeezed
    lemon juice
1 garlic clove, crushed
a pinch of salt
2 tablespoons freshly chopped
    flat-leaf parsley, plus extra
    to garnish
1 fresh red chilli/chile pepper,
    deseeded and finely sliced
300 g/11 oz. precooked octopus
    tentacles, sliced (see page 107
    and Note on this page)
8 razor clams
8 large king prawns/jumbo
    shrimp, shelled
250 g/9 oz. clams
250 g/9 oz. mussels
sea salt flakes, to garnish
chunks of rustic bread, to serve

Serves 4

Put 2 tablespoons of the olive oil in a large bowl with the lemon juice, garlic and salt. Whisk and once emulsified, stir in the flat-leaf parsley and chilli/chile and set aside. You can add the precooked octopus to the bowl now, if using.

Warm the remaining 2 tablespoons of olive oil in a large lidded frying pan/skillet over a high heat. Add the razor clams and prawns/shrimp (and squid if using) to the pan and stir fry for a minute before adding 1 tablespoon of cold water and covering. Let this steam for 1 minute, shaking the pan, until the razor clams open and the prawns/shrimp turn pink. Remove the pan from the heat and transfer the seafood to a clean bowl using a slotted spoon, leaving the cooking juices behind.

Put the pan back over a high heat, add the clams and mussels (if the pan is dry add 1 tablespoon of water) and cover. Cook for a few minutes, just until the mussels and clams have opened, then transfer the shellfish to a separate bowl using a slotted spoon. When the mussels and clams are cool enough to handle, keep a few of each in their shells but remove the flesh from the rest, discarding the shells.

When you are ready to serve, tip all the seafood into the bowl with the dressing and pre-cooked octopus (if using) and fold everything together. Decant all the seafood onto a serving platter using a slotted spoon, and finish with a sprinkling of sea salt flakes, chopped flat-leaf parsley and spoon over any extra dressing if you desire.

Serve with rustic bread and plenty of crisp white wine.

Note: To pre-cook the octopus simply, poach it in a large saucepan/pot of salted boiling water for 35–40 minutes, until tender when pierced with a knife. Remove from the pan, leave it to cool before anointing it with a little olive oil, then cut into bite-sized pieces, leaving the ends of the tentacles intact. You can of course swap octopus for cleaned squid if easier to source; just slice each tube into thirds and cook it at the same time as the razor clams at the start.

GRATITUDE
LIGHTER DISHES FOR SUMMER

BEETROOT, FIG & GRAIN SALAD
WITH GOAT'S CHEESE & HAZELNUT DRESSING

This substantial and delicious salad combines simple ingredients whose flavours and textures all come together effortlessly. Earthy roasted beetroot/beets, creamy goat's cheese and sweet figs, with satisfyingly chewy mixed grains and the peppery notes of rocket/arugula, all finished off with a nutty dressing. It's easy and satisfying to roast your own beetroot but this salad can also be made with unvinegared, pre-cooked ones if that's easier for you. Likewise, a 250-g/9-oz. pouch of prepared mixed grains can be substituted if you find yourself pushed for time.

350 g/¾ lb. raw beetroot/beets, peeled, cut into wedges
6 garlic cloves
a few sprigs of thyme (optional)
a drizzle of olive oil
160 g/1 cup wheat berries
40 g/¼ cup black quinoa
40 g/¼ cup white quinoa
a small handful of rocket/arugula
leaves from a few sprigs each of mint, flat-leaf parsley and coriander/cilantro, torn
50 g/½ cup fresh pomegranate seeds
1 tablespoon freshly squeezed lemon juice
6 fresh figs, sliced
100 g/3½ oz. soft goat's cheese
salt and freshly ground black pepper, to season

For the Hazelnut Dressing
1 tablespoon hazelnut oil
1 tablespoon extra virgin olive oil
1 tablespoon sherry vinegar
3 tablespoons coarsely chopped toasted hazelnuts

Serves 6

Preheat the oven to 180°C fan/200°C/400°F/Gas 6.

To make the Hazelnut Dressing, whisk together the hazelnut oil, extra virgin olive oil and sherry vinegar in a small bowl until emulsified and add the chopped hazelnuts. Season with salt and pepper and set aside.

Place the beetroot/beet wedges, garlic and sprigs of thyme on a baking sheet, coat with a little olive oil, season with salt and pepper then cover with foil. Bake in the preheated oven for about 1 hour. Once cooked, remove from the oven and leave to cool.

Using 3 different saucepans, put the wheat berries in water and boil for about 40–50 minutes until they are soft but still a little chewy, you don't want any crunch. Cook the black quinoa the same way for about 20 minutes and the white quinoa for about 12. Once all the grains are cooked, drain and lay out on a tray to cool and steam dry. Leave the quinoa naked but anoint the wheatberries with a little olive oil and season with salt and pepper whilst still warm.

Once the grains are cooled, place the rocket/arugula, herbs and pomegranate seeds on top, drizzle over a little lemon juice and tip out onto a large serving platter, mixing them together as you do. Scatter over the beetroot/beet and sliced figs, dot chunks of the goat's cheese around the dish and finish by spooning over the Hazelnut Dressing.

CAPONATA WITH POMMES ALIGOT

This classic dish from the island of Sicily soothes with velvety aubergines/
eggplant and plump raisins then surprises you with the *agrodolce* (sour-
sweet) surprise of red wine vinegar and salty capers. I like it served on a
creamy bed of *Pommes Aligot* (see page 126), but it can be eaten on its own,
stirred through cooked pasta or enjoyed as a dip, if that is what you fancy.

2 aubergines/eggplant
100 ml/generous ⅓ cup olive oil
½ medium white onion, diced
2 garlic cloves, sliced
2 ripe tomatoes, deseeded and
    roughly chopped
1 tablespoon red wine vinegar
2 tablespoons raisins
2 heaped tablespoons capers in
    vinegar, drained
2 tablespoons toasted pine nuts
a small handful of coriander/
    cilantro, basil or flat-leaf
    parsley leaves, to garnish
½ fresh red chilli/chile, diced
    (optional)
extra virgin olive oil, to drizzle
salt and freshly ground black
    pepper, to season
1 quantity Pommes Aligot (see
    page 126), to serve

Serves 4

Slice the stalk ends off the aubergines/eggplant, then quarter them
lengthways and cut them into chunks, each about 5 cm/2 inches wide.

Add a generous splash of olive oil to a large saucepan and set over
a high heat. Add the aubergine/eggplant chunks and fry/sauté until
golden on both sides, turning just once. Remove from the pan and
set aside on a plate lined with paper towels.

Reduce the heat under the pan and add the onion, with another
splash of olive oil if needed. Fry/sauté the onion for a few minutes just
to soften it, then add the garlic and cook for another 2 minutes before
adding the tomatoes and vinegar. Let the vinegar reduce for 1 minute,
then season generously with salt and pepper.

Return the fried aubergine/eggplant chunks to the pan. Add the
raisins and capers along with 1 tablespoon of water. Simmer gently,
uncovered, for about 10 minutes until cooked through; try not to stir
so as to avoid breaking the aubergines/eggplant up too much.

To serve, top with the pine nuts, basil, chilli/chile (if using) and
drizzle with extra virgin olive oil.

Serve hot or at room temperature, spooned on top of the Pommes
Aligot, or however you want to enjoy it.

MEATLESS MOUSSAKA

Famous the world over, moussaka's layers of rich meat ragù, potato and aubergine/eggplant, topped with a white sauce, are a labour of love to create, but worth the effort. My veggie version is just as delicious and I serve it with a simply dressed green salad. The contrast of sharp vinaigrette with a forkful of creamy moussaka always reminds me of dinner at my mum and dad's.

olive oil, for frying/sautéing
300 g/10½ oz. waxy potatoes
2 aubergines/eggplant
2 courgettes/zucchini
a few pinches of Greek dried
    oregano
25 g/¼ cup grated vegetarian
    Parmesan-style hard cheese
salt and freshly ground black
    pepper, to season

For the vegetable ragù
1 kg/2¼ lb. mushrooms, diced
1 medium white onion, diced
2 garlic cloves, chopped
150 g/2 cups precooked brown
    lentils
3 tablespoons tomato purée/paste
a handful of flat-leaf parsley
    leaves, chopped
½ tablespoon ground cinnamon
12 grates of nutmeg
1 tablespoon Greek dried
    oregano
1 teaspoon soft dark brown sugar

For the béchamel sauce
75 g/¾ stick unsalted butter
75 g/½ cup plus 1 tablespoon
    plain/all-purpose flour
600 ml/2½ cups whole milk

*a 30 x 20-cm/12 x 8-inch
    ovenproof baking dish*

Serves 4

Preheat the oven to 180°C fan/200°C/400°F/Gas 6.

Peel the potatoes and cut them into 5-mm/¼-inch thick slices. Cut the aubergines/eggplant and zucchini/courgettes into 1-cm ½-inch thick slices.

Line a tray with paper towels. Heat a splash of oil in a large frying pan/skillet set over a medium heat. Add the potato, aubergine/eggplant and courgette/zucchini slices in batches and fry/sauté until golden and just cooked through, then transfer to the paper towel-lined tray to drain. Arrange a layer of potato slices in the baking dish, and season with a pinch of oregano and a few grinds of black pepper. Repeat with a layer of aubergine/eggplant and finally courgette/zucchini, again adding oregano and seasoning between each layer.

To make the ragù, add a little oil to a medium saucepan and set over a high heat. Add the mushrooms and fry/sauté for about 15 minutes, stirring occasionally; you want these deeply caramel coloured. Turn down the heat and add the onion and cook through for another 5 minutes until it has softened and coloured. Add the garlic and cook for 1 minute, then add the lentils, tomato purée/paste, parsley, cinnamon, nutmeg, oregano and sugar. Add about 60 ml/¼ cup of water and simmer, uncovered, for 10–15 minutes until the ragù is rich and thick. Spoon this over the layered vegetables, levelling the surface with the back of the spoon.

To make the béchamel sauce, melt the butter in a saucepan set over a low-medium heat. Add the flour and stir continuously until a paste forms and cook this for 2 minutes. Add the milk to the pan gradually, whisking/beating as you go, until the sauce has thickened and is smooth. Season generously with salt and pepper.

Gently pour the sauce over the ragù layer, again smoothing out the surface with the back of a spoon. Scatter the grated cheese over the top and cook into the preheated oven for 30 minutes. Leave to rest for 15 minutes before serving with a simply dressed green salad.

WHITE BEAN FASOLIA
WITH PIMENTÓN-ROASTED VEGETABLES

This crushed white bean salad laced with lemon juice and olive oil is a Cypriot classic made from staple village ingredients. Adding smoky roasted vegetables in a spicy dressing brings flavour and more substance to the dish.

400-g/14-oz. can each of haricot/navy beans and cannellini beans, drained and rinsed
1 fresh green chilli/chile, deseeded and sliced
a handful each of flat-leaf parsley and coriander/cilantro leaves
finely grated zest and freshly squeezed juice of 1 lemon
4 tablespoons extra virgin olive oil
a few toasted whole almonds, lightly crushed
salt and freshly ground black pepper, to season

For the Pimentón-roasted Vegetables
1 garlic clove, crushed
1 fresh red chilli/chile, deseeded and finely chopped
1 tablespoon runny honey
freshly squeezed juice of 1 lemon
4 tablespoons tomato purée/paste
100 ml/generous ⅓ cup olive oil, plus extra to drizzle
1 aubergine/eggplant, cut lengthways into 8 wedges
2 courgettes/zucchini, cut lengthways into 4 wedges
2 small red onions, quartered
4 Portobello mushrooms, peeled
1 tablespoon sweet Spanish smoked paprika (pimentón dulce)
a pinch of ground cumin

Serves 4

Preheat the oven to 200°C fan/220°C/425°F/Gas 7.

To make the dressing for the Pimentón-roasted Vegetables, pulverize the garlic and fresh red chilli/chile in a pestle and mortar, adding a pinch of salt to act as an abrasive. Add the honey, lemon juice and tomato purée/paste and mix together, ensuring the garlic is completely crushed and incorporated into the dressing; it will be a paste-like consistency. Scrape the paste into a large bowl and whisk in the olive oil. It should now be a pouring consistency so add a splash of water if it's too thick. Set aside.

Put all the prepared vegetables on a baking sheet, ensuring it is not overcrowded. Drizzle over some olive oil, season with salt and pepper and dust with the smoked paprika and cumin. Roast in the preheated oven for about 20 minutes, until the vegetables are just soft but not mushy (check them by prodding with a knife after 15 minutes). Once cooked, tip the vegetables into the bowl with dressing, and toss them to coat.

To make the Fasolia, put the haricot/navy beans in a bowl and lightly crush them with a spatula or potato masher, just gently to break them up. Fold in the cannellini beans, sliced fresh green chilli/chile, parsley, coriander/cilantro (reserving some herbs to garnish), lemon zest and juice and the extra virgin olive oil. Season generously with salt and pepper and transfer to a serving bowl.

Stack the dressed roasted vegetables on top of the fasolia, pouring over any pan juices from the baking sheet or remaining dressing from the bowl. Garnish with the reserved herbs and the crushed toasted almonds and serve.

ANCHOVY SPAGHETTI
WITH PINE NUT PICADA

This is my take on a classic pasta dish that only uses a handful of ingredients but nonetheless captures the flavours of Sicily. Traditionally it is paired with crispy *Pangritata* (see page 130) but here instead I've taken my inspiration from Spain with a drier than usual version of *Picada*, a dense, pounded paste of fried bread, nuts, garlic and olive oil that originated in the Catalonia region as a way to thicken and flavour stews. Almonds are traditional, but some recipes call for hazelnuts, walnuts or pine nuts, as I've used here. You can serve this without my picada-style topping, but just remember to lift it with some chopped flat-leaf parsley and a squeeze of lemon juice instead.

350 g/12 oz. fresh spaghetti
   or 200 g/7 oz. dried (or any
   other pasta of your choice)
100 ml/generous ⅓ cup olive oil
a small knob/pat of butter
12 anchovy fillets in olive oil,
   drained
2 garlic cloves, thinly sliced
8 cherry tomatoes, quartered
a pinch of dried chilli/hot red
   pepper flakes
salt and freshly ground black
   pepper, to season

For the Pine Nut Picada
50 g/scant ½ cup pine nuts
2 tablespoons olive oil
1 slice of day-old bread, coarsely
   chopped
2 tablespoons finely chopped
   flat-leaf parsley leaves
1 garlic clove, crushed
finely grated zest of ½ a lemon

Serves 4

First make the Picada. Toast the pine nuts in a dry frying pan/skillet for a couple of minutes, then pulverize them in a food processor or pestle and mortar until the texture of coarse sand. Put in a small bowl.

Line a plate with paper towels. Add the oil to the same pan and fry/sauté the bread until golden. Tip onto the paper towel-lined plate to drain and then add to the bowl with the pine nuts and crush them just a little with a pestle or the back of a spoon. Add the parsley, garlic and lemon zest to the bowl and stir to combine; it will be quite dry which is what we want for this particular dish. Set aside until needed.

Cook the pasta according to the package instructions – you can put it on now if you are using dried pasta. If using fresh pasta, do it later, once the sauce has been made.

Add the oil and butter to a large saucepan set over a medium-hot heat. Add the anchovy fillets and stir – they will start to melt into the oil. Just before the anchovies have totally dissolved, add the garlic and tomatoes (crushing the tomatoes in the pan with a fork to release their juices). Cook for a few minutes, until the tomatoes have just started to soften then remove from the heat and add the dried chilli/hot red pepper flakes.

Drain the pasta and return it to the pan. Add the anchovy, oil and tomato mixture and heat for a few minutes, just to help the pasta absorb all the lovely flavours. Season with a little salt (the anchovies are already pretty salty!) and pepper. Spoon the dressed pasta into bowls and sprinkle the picada over the top of each one to serve.

JEWELLED STUFFED SARDINES

We should all eat more sardines. They're incredibly good for you, cheap and sustainable. Eaten throughout the Mediterranean, one of my favourite things to eat is the whole fish grilled until the skin is crisp and served with nothing more than a squeeze of lemon juice and a glass of wine. These Sicilian-style stuffed sardines once again use the humblest of ingredients to create something delicious. Old bread, lemons and orange zest, a handful of sweet raisins... they are a delight. I've said here that this will serve four people, but I'd be lying if I said I haven't polished off a plateful all by myself...

16 fresh whole sardines, scaled and gutted by your fishmonger
40 g/scant ¼ cup raisins
45 ml/3 tablespoons white wine
80 g/1½ cups fresh breadcrumbs (see page 130), made from a dry, stale loaf
a small pinch of white sugar
a small handful of flat-leaf parsley leaves, chopped
finely grated zest of ½ an orange
finely grated zest of 1 lemon, plus lemon wedges for squeezing
3 tablespoons flaked/slivered almonds, lightly toasted
2 tablespoons olive oil, plus extra for greasing

Serves 4

First fillet the sardines. To do this, open out the gutted fish and place skin-side up on your work surface. Holding the tail with one hand, firmly press along the backbone with the other until the fish is completely flat. Turn the fish over and gently pull away the backbone. If the head is still attached, use scissors to snip where the backbone begins before you start. Keep pulling until you reach the tail end, then cut off the backbone and discard. Scrape away any remaining small bones. Cut each butterflied fish in half to make 2 fillets ready to stuff.

Preheat the oven to 220°C fan/240°C/475°F/Gas 9.

Put the raisins in a small heatproof bowl. Warm the wine in a small saucepan set over a low heat and pour it over the raisins. Leave them to steep; you want them to be nice and plump.

Toast the breadcrumbs in a dry frying pan/skillet for a few minutes just until crisp, you don't need to colour them. Remove from the heat and let cool in the pan for a minute before tipping into a mixing bowl. Add all the other ingredients, including the olive oil, and drain and stir in the raisins last. Mix to combine.

Lightly oil a baking sheet. Lay a sardine fillet skin-side down on your work surface. Take a small amount of stuffing, about a heaped tablespoon, and gently press it together with your fingers to form a piece about the same size as the sardine and put this on the fillet. Lay another fillet flesh-side down on top of the stuffing and pat it down a little, to make a sardine sandwich, with the stuffing as the filling. Transfer to the baking sheet and repeat until all the sardines are stuffed. Sprinkle over any unused stuffing and put in the preheated oven for about 8 minutes, or until the sardines are cooked through.

Lay the stuffed sardines on a platter and serve with lemon wedges.

OVEN ROASTED HAKE ON CITRUSY GREENS

Hake is a deliciously sweet and clean-tasting white fish found throughout the Mediterranean and is also one of the UK's most sustainable. Unfortunately it doesn't make it onto our kitchen tables as much as the so-called 'big five' (haddock, cod, tuna, salmon and prawns/shrimp) and it should! The first time I cooked this recipe was in the south of France for a staff lunch when asparagus was in season and I had just bought a bunch from a roadside stall outside someone's home. In fact, it was just an old broken wooden stall laden with packs of asparagus and a pot to leave the money in. This dish was such a hit that it's been a staple for our summer lunches there ever since. Crisp, lightly roasted green vegetables enveloped in a wine, butter and lemon dressing with the roasted fish resting on top, it's simple and for me, beautiful, and best of all, it's all cooked in the oven in one pan.

250 g/8 oz. on-the-vine cherry tomatoes

200 g/7 oz. fine green/French beans, trimmed

3 garlic cloves, sliced

200 ml/¾ cup white wine

60 ml/⅓ cup olive oil

200 g/4 scant cups fresh spinach leaves, washed and stemmed

200 g/7 oz. fresh asparagus spears, trimmed

250 g/2 cups frozen petit pois

2 lemons, each cut into quarters

60 g/½ stick butter

4 x 200-g/7-oz. hake fillets, skinned

2 tablespoons each of chopped flat-leaf parsley and dill

salt and freshly ground black pepper, to season

boiled new potatoes, to serve (optional)

Serves 4

Preheat the oven to 200°C fan/220°C/425°F/Gas 7.

Snip the vines of the cherry tomatoes with kitchen scissors to make four roughly even-sized pieces. Put them on a baking sheet, drizzle with a little olive oil and season with salt and pepper. Bake in the preheated oven for 10–12 minutes, just to warm them through and split the skins slightly. Set aside.

Put the beans and garlic in a large, deep-sided roasting pan. Pour over the wine and add a splash of olive oil. Mix together and bake in the preheated oven for 10 minutes then remove.

Next add the spinach leaves and toss them with the beans so that they will wilt slightly from the heat. Follow with the asparagus and petit pois and toss again to combine. Squeeze the juice from the lemon wedges over the vegetables and drop them into the pan. Season generously with salt and pepper, drizzle over a little more olive oil and dot half the butter over the vegetables.

Place the hake fillets on top of the vegetables, season with salt and pepper and put a small piece of the remaining butter on each one.

Return the pan to the hot oven and roast for a further 7–10 minutes, until the flesh flakes easily.

To serve, add the roasted tomatoes to the pan, scatter over the chopped parsley and dill and take the whole pan to the table. Serve with boiled new potatoes, if liked.

WHOLE TURBOT OVEN-ROASTED
WITH FENNEL, NEW POTATOES & TOMATO

Turbot is a beautiful meaty white fish. Roasted whole on the bone and carved at the table, this is one of those village-style celebration dishes, by which I mean something large cooked for a rowdy group to share! Here my turbot rests on a bed of roasted fennel, tender new potatoes and baby plum tomatoes that melt into a silky duvet to be mopped up by the fish. I love this served with a light chicken broth gravy; completely untraditional but it works. If you'd rather keep the dish pescatarian, just swap out the chicken stock for a good vegetable bouillon.

1 kg/2¼ lb. new potatoes

60 g/½ stick butter

½ teaspoon fennel seeds

1 teaspoon coriander seeds

1 teaspoon paprika

leaves stripped from 3 sprigs of thyme, plus a few extra sprigs

1.2–1.5-kg/2¾–3-lb. whole fresh turbot, on the bone

6 dried bay leaves

2 tablespoons chopped flat-leaf parsley

400 g/14 oz. Tenderstem broccoli/broccolini

6 spring onions/scallions, left whole

2 fennel bulbs, trimmed and thinly sliced

200 g/7 oz. baby plum tomatoes

3 garlic cloves, sliced

100 ml/generous ⅓ cup white wine

250 ml/1 cup light chicken stock

1 tablespoon cornflour/cornstarch

olive oil, to drizzle

salt and freshly ground black pepper, to season

Serves 6

Preheat the oven to 200°C fan/220°C/425°F/Gas 7.

Put the potatoes in a large saucepan of salted water to cover and bring them to the boil. Cook for about 15 minutes, until just cooked with a little resistance when pricked with a fork. Drain and fold in a knob/pat of the butter and season with a pinch of salt. Put the buttered potatoes in the centre of a large, deep-sided roasting pan.

Toast the fennel and coriander seeds in a dry frying pan/skillet for 1 minute, then tip them into a pestle and mortar and crush them. Mix with the paprika, thyme leaves and a little salt and freshly ground black pepper.

Lightly oil the turbot and use a sharp knife to score three shallow slits in the flesh on each side of the centre bone. Insert a bay leaf into each slit and sprinkle the ground spice and thyme mixture over the fish. Put it on top of the potatoes in the roasting pan, finishing with sprinkling the chopped parsley over the whole tray.

Arrange the broccoli, spring onions/scallions, fennel and tomatoes around the fish and sprinkle over the garlic slices and a couple of thyme sprigs.

Pour the wine into the pan from one side, dot the remaining butter around the pan and roast in the preheated oven for 25–30 minutes, or until the turbot is cooked (it will start to pull away from the bones).

Remove the pan from the oven. Gently pour out or spoon any pan juices into a saucepan and cover the fish loosely with foil. Add the chicken stock to the saucepan (topping up with water if you want more gravy!). Mix the cornflour/cornstarch with a little cold water to make a slurry and pour into the saucepan, bring to a simmer stirring until it thickens, pour into a gravy jug/small pitcher.

To serve, take the whole pan to the table and serve the sauce alongside for pouring.

FIERY CLAM & LENTIL SKILLET

Clams are not only a tasty treat but also highly sustainable and this deliciously easy skillet supper combines them with earthy Puy/French green lentils for a hearty dish laced with smoky notes and fresh herbs.

200 g/7 oz. small, on-the-vine tomatoes
olive oil, for drizzling and frying/sautéing
150 g/1 scant cup dried Puy/French green lentils
3 garlic cloves, 1 whole, 2 crushed
2 dried bay leaves
a sprig of thyme
1 medium white onion, diced
1 fresh red chilli/chile, deseeded and finely diced
1 teaspoon smoked paprika
2 tablespoons tomato purée/paste
1 kg/2¼ lb. fresh clams
60 ml/¼ cup white wine
a handful of flat-leaf parsley leaves, chopped
a few squeezes of fresh lemon juice
salt and freshly ground black pepper, to season

Serves 4

Preheat oven to 180°C fan/200°C/400°F/Gas 6.

Leave the tomatoes attached to the vine and put them on a baking sheet, drizzle with a little olive oil and season with salt and pepper. Bake them in the preheated oven for 15 minutes, until their skins start to split. Set aside.

Put the lentils in a saucepan and pour in about 750 ml/3 cups of cold water (it should be three times the volume of the lentils) and set over a medium heat. Add the whole garlic clove, bay leaves and thyme sprig to the pan and simmer for 25 minutes, or until the lentils are just cooked through. Drain and reserve.

Add a splash of olive oil to a heavy frying pan/large skillet and set over a medium heat. Add the onion and fry/sauté until it starts to caramelize, then add the crushed garlic cloves and chilli/chile. After 1 minute add the smoked paprika and tomato purée/paste followed by the clams. Stir to combine everything, then pour in the wine. Increase the heat to high, cover the pan with a lid, and cook until the clams open, shaking the pan periodically. Remove the lid and simmer to reduce the cooking liquor for 1 minute, then fold through the cooked lentils and simmer for a few minutes only, until the liquor has thickened and reduced further. Remove from the heat and rest for 5 minutes.

To serve, dot the roasted tomatoes on top of the clams, scatter over some chopped flat-leaf parsley and add a squeeze of lemon juice and a little salt and pepper to season, if needed.

PORK & FENNEL
GEM LETTUCE CUPS

Pork and fennel are long established flavour friends. Here minced/ground pork is combined with toasted fennel seeds and fresh summery herbs as well as orzo pasta (which gives a softer and more filling texture) and then spooned into crisp lettuce leaves; these are delicious and have proved to be a great mezze dish for sharing, or if you're the jealous type, just devour them between the two of you.

750 ml/3 cups hot chicken stock (made with 1 stock/bouillon cube)
50 g/½ cup dried orzo pasta
olive oil, for frying/sautéing and drizzling
1 tablespoon fennel seeds
500 g/18 oz. minced/ground pork
1 fresh red chilli/chile, deseeded and finely chopped
2 garlic cloves, sliced
a generous pinch of dried oregano
freshly squeezed juice of ½ a lemon
2 Little Gem/baby Cos or romaine lettuce heads
a small handful each of coriander/cilantro and mint leaves, torn
salt and freshly ground black pepper, to season

Serves 2 (or 4 as a sharer)

Put the hot chicken stock in a large saucepan set over a medium heat. Add the orzo pasta, bring it to the boil and cook until just soft. Drain, return to the pan and splash over a little olive oil to stop it sticking and set aside.

Toast the fennel seeds over a medium heat in dry frying pan/skillet for 30 seconds, then remove them from the pan and set aside.

Add a splash of olive oil to the same pan, increase the heat to high and add the minced/ground pork. Fry/sauté, stirring, until it is almost cooked and then add the chilli/chile (keeping a little back to garnish), garlic, oregano and toasted fennel seeds. Continue cooking for 3–5 minutes, until the meat is slightly coloured. Just before you remove the pan from the heat, season generously with salt and pepper, add the lemon juice and fold in the cooked orzo. Remove from the heat and let rest while you prepare the lettuce leaves.

To do this, trim off the stalk end and peel away the biggest leaves. Arrange them facing upright on a serving dish to create cups. Fold the torn coriander/cilantro and mint through the minced/ground pork and orzo mixture, keeping a little back to garnish, and spoon it equally amongst the lettuce cups.

Garnish with the reserved chopped chilli/chile and herbs and serve.

LEMON GOAT 'EN PAPILLOTE'

Something of a Trojan horse... *en papillote*, the French term for cooking food in a parcel of parchment or foil, is in this instance concealing Hellenic notes of lemon, oregano, sweet prunes and goat neck fillets, slow cooked for a meltingly delicious gift-wrapped meal. This recipe serves two, but simply double up if you need a meal for four people. If goat is not your thing, this recipe also works brilliantly with lamb neck fillets (but they must be fillets, not neck with the bone).

olive oil, to drizzle
60 g/⅓ cup dried yellow split
    peas
2 new potatoes, thinly sliced
4 small spring onions/scallions,
    whole
10 fine green/French beans,
    trimmed
3 soft, pitted prunes, halved
2 ripe tomatoes, thinly sliced
2 garlic cloves, chopped
125 ml/½ cup dry rosé or
    white wine
2 teaspoons Greek dried oregano
400 g/14 oz. goat neck fillet
60 ml/¼ cup passata (Italian
    sieved/strained tomatoes)
2 teaspoons butter
finely grated zest of 2 lemons,
    plus lemon wedges to serve
a few pinches of chopped
    flat-leaf parsley
salt and freshly ground black
    pepper, to season
chunks of rustic bread, to serve

baking parchment

kitchen foil

Serves 2

Preheat the oven to 160°C fan/180°C/350°F/Gas 4.

Begin by cutting out 2 pieces each of foil and baking parchment, both about 45-cm/18-inches square. Lay out the sheets of foil and place the baking parchment on top (ready to fill and parcel up).

Drizzle a little olive oil in the middle of each square of baking parchment, pile half the yellow split peas in the centre of each one followed by half the potato slices, 2 of the spring onions/scallions (bent in half), half the fine beans and half the sliced prunes in each parcel and a sliced tomato in each, reserving a slice of tomato to put on top of the meat. Add 1 garlic clove to each one and then pour half the wine into each. Dust each with a pinch of oregano and season with salt and pepper.

Season the goat neck fillets all over with salt and pepper and dust with the remaining oregano. Put them on top of the piles of vegetables. Spoon half the passata/Italian strained tomatoes over each one, dot with a little butter, sprinkle the zest of 1 lemon into each and finish with a pinch of chopped flat-leaf parsley.

Bring the sides of the baking parchment together to form packages, twist the ends so they are sealed and fold the tops over by 2.5 cm/1 inch. Bring up the edges of the underlying foil and hug it around the package, holding it all in place.

Cook in the preheated oven on a wire pizza rack on top of a baking sheet (to help the hot air circulate under the parcel) for 3 hours. Once cooked, remove from the oven and let rest for at least 15 minutes unopened, by which time the goat will be rested and tender.

Put the parcel in a shallow serving bowl with some lemon wedges for squeezing. Serve with some rustic bread to mop up the juices. .

MACARONIA POLI
WITH CRISPY CHICKEN SKIN

This dish is enveloped in childhood memories for me... macaroni cooked in a slow-poached chicken stock and served with a grating of halloumi cheese; simple, delicious and utterly satisfying. The recipe has its roots in peasant food so originally an old hen, only good for stock, would be used rather than a young bird. To add my own twist, I like to fry the chicken skin until it's nice and crispy and scatter over the top for a little crunch. The carcass of the chicken can then be used again to make another stock if you want to fully embrace the frugal nature of the dish!

360 g/3 cups dried macaroni
 pasta
125 g/1 cup frozen peas or
 petit pois
olive oil, for frying/sautéing
halloumi cheese, for grating

For the chicken stock
1 small cornfed chicken (about
 1.2 kg/2¼ lb.)
1 small white onion halved,
 skin on
2 garlic cloves, peeled and
 left whole
2 dried bay leaves
a pinch of Greek dried oregano
a few sprigs of flat-leaf parsley
salt and freshly ground black
 pepper, to season

Serves 4

Put 1.5 litres/6 cups of cold water in a very large saucepan or ideally a stock pot. Add the whole chicken, along with the onion, garlic, bay leaves, oregano and parsley. Set the pot over a medium-high heat and bring the pot to a bubbling simmer; don't boil it though as it will go tough, a slow poach is what you're aiming for. Once bubbling, skim off any impurities from the surface of the water with a ladle, reduce the heat to a gentle simmer and leave to poach for about 1–1½ hours, until the juices run clear when the chicken thigh is pierced with a knife.

Once cooked, turn off the heat and leave the chicken to rest in the stock for 30 minutes. When you're ready, take out the chicken and leave it covered in a bowl. Pass the stock through a sieve/strainer.

Cook the macaroni following the package instructions but replace the water with the chicken stock. A few minutes before it's ready, add the peas to the pan. Once they bob to the surface of the water, drain the pasta.

While the macaroni is cooking, strip the skin from the chicken, coarsely chop (it will be a little tacky but persevere, the end result is worth it). Line a plate with paper towels. Set a frying pan/skillet over a high heat and add a splash of olive oil. Fry/sauté the chicken skin for about 8 minutes, until golden and crispy. Season generously with salt and pepper and tip onto the paper towel-lined plate to drain.

When you are ready to serve, finely shred the chicken flesh and fold it through the cooked pasta and peas. Finish by finely grating some halloumi cheese over the top, season, and crumble some of the crispy chicken skin on top.

COMFORT
WARMING FOOD FOR WINTER

TRUFFLED RIBOLLITA

Ribollita is a hearty Tuscan soup traditionally made with whatever vegetables are to hand but always including the locally grown kale known as *cavolo nero* (literally black cabbage). Thickened with chunks of day-old bread and cannellini beans, its earthy nature pairs incredibly well with the truffles that Tuscany is also famous for. A luxury ingredient, truffles might seem decadent in a book about humble food but when in season, they are plentiful and celebrated at dedicated festivals where gnarly-handed farmers sell the delicate (equally gnarly looking) black and white treasure at their stalls. If you are reading this at home and not wandering around a Tuscan market... a drizzle of truffle oil can be substituted or Parmesan shavings.

120 g/4 oz. day-old sourdough
    bread crusts
olive oil, for frying/sautéing
a pinch of dried oregano
1 large white onion, diced
1 large carrot, diced
1 celery stick/stalk, diced
3 garlic cloves, diced
1 teaspoon fennel seeds
125 ml/½ cup canned chopped
    tomatoes
a pinch of sugar
400-g/14-oz. can cannellini
    beans, drained and rinsed
1 large potato, peeled and cut
    into 1.5 cm/½-inch cubes
750 ml/3 cups vegetable stock
    or water
120 g/4 oz. cavolo nero or chard
salt and freshly ground black
    pepper, to season
extra virgin olive oil (or truffle oil,
    see recipe intro), to drizzle
a few shavings of fresh truffle
    (optional) or Parmesan cheese,
    to serve

Serves 6

Cut 20 g/¾ oz. of the sourdough crusts into 1.5-cm/½-inch cubes. Heat a splash of olive oil in a large frying pan/skillet set over low heat and fry until slightly golden, season with salt and pepper and pinch of dried oregano and set aside to garnish. Cut the remaining bread into 2.5-cm/1-inch cubes and set aside.

Add a splash of olive oil to a large saucepan and set over low heat. Gently sweat the onion, carrot, celery and garlic for about 10 minutes until soft and tender, but not coloured and season with salt and pepper. Add the fennel seeds and stir for 1 minute before adding the tomatoes and sugar. Simmer the mixture, uncovered, for a few more minutes to create a rich base.

Add the cannellini beans and potato, along with the stock or water, and simmer for 5 minutes, or until the potato is tender but not soft. Shred the cavolo nero or chard leaves and put them into the soup, you may have to do this in batches until they have all wilted. Fold in the remaining bread cubes and leave the soup on the heat just long enough for the bread to warm through and soften.

Serve immediately with a drizzle of extra virgin olive oil and topped with the fried bread cubes and some shavings of fresh truffle (if using) or Parmesan on top.

ESPINACAS CON GARBANZOS

This flavoursome Spanish-inspired dish of spinach with chickpeas uses a blend of toasted almonds and spices ground together to thicken the sauce and this gives a richness to an otherwise humble dish. Traditionally a tapas dish, this recipe will serve six, but I also sometimes serve it with a mound of couscous to make it a hearty main meal for two.

olive oil, for frying/sautéing
1 large white onion, finely diced
400 g/14 oz. fresh spinach leaves, washed and larger stems sliced
1 teaspoon coriander seeds
25 g/¼ cup whole blanched almonds
1 garlic clove, coarsely chopped
½ slice day-old rustic bread, chopped
1 teaspoon ground cumin
1 teaspoon Spanish sweet smoked paprika (pimentón dulce)
¼ teaspoon salt
1 tablespoon sherry vinegar
400-g/14-oz. can chickpeas, drained and rinsed
½ tablespoon tomato purée/paste
1 large ripe tomato, deseeded and finely diced
120 ml/½ cup hot water
extra virgin olive oil, to drizzle
freshly squeezed lemon juice
salt and freshly ground black pepper, to season

To serve (optional)
150 g/1 scant cup dried couscous
1 tablespoon extra virgin olive oil

a pestle and mortar

Serves 2

Put the couscous (if using), into a heatproof bowl, add the extra virgin olive oil and pour in sufficient just-boiled water to sit about 1.5 cm/½ inch above the couscous. Cover the bowl with a plate and leave for 15 minutes, then fluff with a fork (only ever a fork, a spoon will turn it into sludge). Season generously with salt and pepper and set aside until ready to serve.

Add a splash of olive oil to a large frying pan/skillet and set over a low heat. Fry/sauté the onion for about 10 minutes, until it has caramelized, then tip onto a plate and set aside. Add another little splash of oil to the pan and fry/sauté the spinach and any stalks in batches until it is wilted. Transfer to a sieve/strainer set over a bowl to catch any liquid (you can discard this).

Wipe the pan with paper towels and lightly toast the coriander seeds until just fragrant. Crush in a mortar with a pestle and reserve to garnish. Add the whole almonds to the pan and toast until they colour slightly, then add a splash of olive oil and once hot add the garlic and bread. Fry/sauté until the bread is crispy and then add the cumin, pimentón and salt and mix to coat everything. Remove from the heat, reserve about 6 whole toasted almonds to garnish, and spoon the rest of the mixture into a pestle and mortar. Crush, adding the vinegar a little at a time as you go, to form a paste.

Add another little splash of olive oil to the pan and set over medium heat. Add the chickpeas, tomato purée/paste and crushed almond paste and fry/sauté for 1 minute before adding the fresh tomato and hot water. Simmer until the liquid has reduced and there is just enough to coat the chickpeas; it should be the consistency of single/light cream.

Fold the spinach and onions back into the chickpea mixture. Finish with a few grinds of black pepper, a drizzle of extra virgin olive oil, a squeeze of lemon juice and scatter over the toasted coriander seeds and reserved almonds. Serve with the couscous.

RICH MUSHROOM RAGÙ
ON PARMESAN POLENTA

This dish is inspired by the humble food prepared in Italian villages and designed to feed a large family. I see creamy polenta tipped out directly onto a wooden board and topped with a hearty mushroom ragù, a scene that conjures up romantic notions of what it is to really eat together... But I'm sure my reality would be kids mucking about and adults shouting to be heard over the cacophony! The Parmesan Polenta on page 126 makes the perfect accompaniment here and to a variety of other dishes, especially those with a little sauce looking for something soft to mingle with.

7 g/¼ oz. dried porcini
   mushrooms
olive oil, for frying/sautéing
1 medium white onion, diced
500 g/1 lb. 2 oz. chestnut or
   button mushrooms, halved
2 garlic cloves, sliced
1 teaspoon ground cumin
1 teaspoon smoked paprika
a small pinch of cayenne pepper
1 medium, ripe tomato, deseeded
   and diced
400-g/14-oz. can chickpeas,
   drained and rinsed
100 ml/scant ½ cup white wine
100 ml/scant ½ cup chicken or
   vegetable stock
a knob/pat of butter (optional)
200 g/3 cups fresh mixed wild
   mushrooms, cleaned
1 teaspoon freshly squeezed
   lemon juice
a handful of flat-leaf parsley
   leaves, to garnish
salt and freshly ground black
   pepper, to season
1 quantity Parmesan Polenta
   (see page 126)

Serves 6

Put the dried porcini mushrooms in a heatproof measuring jug/pitcher and top up with 100 ml/scant ½ cup of just-boiled water. Leave to steep for 10 minutes, then drain (reserving the steeping liquid) and squeeze out as much moisture from the mushrooms as possible. Coarsely chop the mushrooms and set aside. Strain the steeping liquid to remove any sediment and set aside.

Set a large, heavy-based frying pan/skillet over low heat and add a splash of olive oil. Add the onion and fry/sauté for 2 minutes, then turn up the heat and add the chestnut mushrooms. Fry/sauté until these are golden, then stir in the soaked porcini mushrooms along with the garlic, cumin, paprika and cayenne pepper.

Add the tomato, chickpeas and wine, and simmer to reduce the wine until it has almost all gone. Pour the reserved mushroom steeping liquid into the pan along with the stock. Simmer until the liquid reduces by two-thirds and thickens to the consistency of single/light cream, then remove the pan from the heat, beat in the butter (if using) and season generously with salt and pepper.

Heat a dry frying pan/skillet until smoking hot. Add a small splash of olive oil, quickly followed by the wild mushrooms and fry/sauté for 1 minute, season generously with salt and pepper, add the lemon juice, then remove from the heat.

To serve, gently reheat the polenta, stirring continuously, and pour it onto a large board or platter, making an indentation in the centre with the back of a spoon and spoon in the mushroom ragù. Scatter the wild mushrooms over the top, along with the flat-leaf parsley.

SPICED CAULIFLOWER STEAKS
WITH ORZO & ROMESCO SAUCE

Here thick-cut cauli steaks are dusted in warming spices and oven roasted along with the leaves that are so often overlooked and wasted, and it's all served on a bed of simply cooked orzo pasta and topped with a moreish red pepper and toasted walnut Romesco sauce.

1 teaspoon smoked paprika
a pinch of cayenne pepper
1 teaspoon ground cumin
1 tablespoon coriander seeds, coarsely crushed
2 tablespoons pine nuts
1 large cauliflower head
olive oil, to drizzle
150 g/1½ cups dried orzo pasta
leaves from a few sprigs of flat-leaf parsley, half chopped, half torn
salt and freshly ground black pepper, to season

For the Romesco Sauce
1 slice of white bread
50 g/generous ⅓ cup walnut halves
1 garlic clove, unpeeled
80 ml/⅓ cup extra virgin olive oil
100 g/3½ oz. roasted red (bell) peppers from a jar
25 g/1 oz. sun-dried tomatoes
a pinch of sugar
1 tablespoon tomato purée/paste
a generous pinch of smoked paprika
salt and freshly ground black pepper, to season

Serves 4

To make the Romesco Sauce, preheat the oven to 160°C fan/ 180°C/350°F/Gas 4. Put the bread, walnuts and garlic on a baking sheet and bake in the preheated oven for about 8–10 minutes. Gently rub the walnuts to remove the skin but don't worry too much about getting it all off. Pour two thirds of the extra virgin olive oil into a food processor along with all the other ingredients (making sure you peel the garlic and trim the stalk end off). Pulse until fairly smooth, season to taste with salt and pepper and fold in the remaining oil. Spoon into a small bowl, cover and chill until ready to serve.

Increase the oven temperature to 180°C fan/200°C/400°F/Gas 6. Put the smoked paprika, cayenne, cumin and coriander seeds in a small bowl and add a generous pinch of salt and a few grinds of pepper. Mix to combine and set aside. Toast the pine nuts in a dry frying pan/skillet set over a low heat, until lightly golden and set aside.

Strip the cauliflower of its leaves, discard any that are wilted and floppy and spread the rest out on a baking sheet. Drizzle with a little olive oil and season with salt and pepper. Set aside.

Slice the cauliflower into 4 steaks, each about 4 cm/1½ inches thick. Coat the cauliflower steaks and any offcuts in a little olive oil, dust in the spice mix and put the whole lot on a large baking sheet. Roast in the preheated oven for about 30 minutes, until the edges have crisped up and their thickest parts are tender. About 15 minutes into the cooking time, put the baking sheet of leaves in the oven too and cook for about 15 minutes until the edges have just coloured.

Cook the orzo until al dente according to the package instructions (this will take around 8 minutes). Once the orzo is cooked, remove it from the heat, drain, add the chopped parsley and a drizzle of olive oil and season generously with salt and pepper. Spoon the orzo onto a serving dish, add the cauliflower leaves and arrange the cauliflower steaks on top. Add the torn parsley leaves, spoon over some Romesco Sauce, scatter with the pine nuts and serve.

CHARRED SQUID WITH NDUJA DRESSING
ON RISOTTO BIANCO

Nduja is a soft, spreadable fermented pork salami, spiced with fiery
Calabrian chilli/chile and here it makes a brilliant dressing. You could just
serve the dressed squid on its own as a small plate with some rustic bread to
mop up the juices, but it also works as a substantial meal when served with
my simple risotto bianco. This super-easy way to cook Arborio rice requires
much less effort than a traditional stirred risotto and although very plain,
it is the perfect canvas for the punchy nduja dressing and charred squid,
from both a flavour and visual point of view. You want a nice, clear vegetable
stock so use a good quality bouillon powder to make it.

4 medium whole squid, cleaned
    (800 g/1¾ lb. total weight)
1 garlic clove, crushed
a pinch of dried oregano
2 tablespoons olive oil
a squeeze of lemon juice
salt and freshly ground black
    pepper, to season

For the Risotto Bianco
675 ml/2¾ cups vegetable stock,
    divided as 500 ml/2 cups and
    175 ml/¾ cup
200 g/1 cup uncooked Arborio/
    risotto rice
1½ tablespoons unsalted butter
salt and freshly ground black
    pepper, to season
1 tablespoon chopped toasted
    walnuts, to garnish (optional)

For the Nduja Dressing
2 tablespoons extra virgin
    olive oil
4 tablespoons nduja
leaves from a sprig of flat-leaf
    parsley, chopped

Serves 4

To make the Nduja Dressing, warm the extra virgin olive oil in a small
saucepan set over a very gentle heat. Add the nduja, stirring with the
back of a spoon until it starts to melt into the oil; don't let it cook, just
melt it. Remove from the heat, add the flat-leaf parsley and set aside.

Next make the risotto. Bring the 500 ml/2 cups of stock to the boil
in a large lidded saucepan, add the rice, cover with the lid and reduce
the heat to a very gentle simmer for 15 minutes. Remove the pan
from the heat and leave the rice undisturbed. Just before you are
ready to serve, fold in the butter and pour the 175 ml/¾ cup of hot
stock in to loosen it and warm it up slightly. Season generously.

While the risotto is simmering away, marinade and cook the squid.
Take a large bowl and add the garlic, oregano, olive oil and lemon
juice. Season with salt and pepper, whisk together and set aside.

Place a wooden spoon inside the cleaned squid and using a sharp
knife, slice 2.5-cm/1-inch slits on the top of the squid (this leaves you
with the top of the squid sliced but the bottom intact). Do this to all
the squid, then put them in the marinade, tentacles and all. Heat a
griddle pan until smoking hot. Shake off the excess marinade from the
squid and lay them flat on the pan a few at a time (don't overcrowd
it). Leave for 1 minute, then start turning a few times until they puff up,
turn white, and are slightly charred but don't overcook them!

Spoon out the loosened risotto onto serving plates, put the squid
on top and spoon the Nduja Dressing over it, drizzling over as much
as you like. Sprinkle with chopped walnuts for extra crunch, if you like.

PAN-FRIED SEA BREAM
WITH ROASTED ENDIVE & ALMOND GREMOLATA

Chicory/Belgian endive takes on an entirely new flavour once cooked as its naturally bitter streak is mellowed and I've accentuated that here with a sweet date butter. It pairs perfectly with sea bream, a delicate white fish and it's finished with a zingy almond gremolata to keep things lively.

3 tablespoons butter
½ tablespoon date molasses
4 white or red chicory/Belgian endive (witloof) heads
olive oil, for roasting and frying/ sautéing
180 g/¾ cup uncooked black rice
2 tablespoons plain/all-purpose flour
4 sea bream fillets, skin-on
leaves from a few sprigs of flat-leaf parsley, chopped
salt and freshly ground black pepper, to season

For the Almond Gremolata
8 whole blanched almonds
4 tablespoons flat-leaf parsley leaves, finely chopped
a pinch of salt
1 garlic clove, crushed
2 tablespoons extra virgin olive oil
finely grated zest of 1 lemon
1 tablespoon freshly squeezed lemon juice

Serves 4

Preheat the oven to 180°C fan/200°C/400°F/Gas 6.

Combine the butter and date molasses in a small saucepan set over a low heat and whisk together to combine. Halve the chicory/Belgian endive heads lengthways and lay them flat on a baking sheet. Drizzle with a little olive oil, brush each one with the date molasses butter and season with salt and pepper. Put in the preheated oven to cook for 20–30 minutes, until wilted and slightly caramelized.

Meanwhile, put the black rice in a sieve/strainer and rinse under cold running water. Tip it into a large saucepan and add 600 ml/ 2½ cups (basically 3 times its volume) of hot water. Set over a medium heat and simmer, uncovered, for about 25–30 minutes, until the rice is just cooked (you want to keep a little bite in it), top up with water during cooking if it starts to evaporate. Drain, season with salt and pepper and drizzle with a little olive oil to stop it sticking together. Set aside.

To make the Almond Gremolata, dry fry the almonds in a small frying pan/skillet set over a low heat until golden. Finely chop them and tip into a bowl. Add all the other ingredients and stir to combine. Cover and set aside.

Generously season the flour with salt and pepper and use it to dust the sea bream fillets. Line a large plate with paper towels. Add a splash of olive oil to a large frying pan/skillet and set over medium heat. Shake the excess flour off 2 of the sea bream fillets and lay them skin-side down in the pan. Fry/sauté for 2 minutes, then turn them over to cook the other sides for 1 further minute. Remove from the pan and put on the paper-towel lined plate whilst you cook the remaining 2 fillets.

To serve, scatter some black rice over each plate, put 2 pieces of roasted chicory/Belgian endive on top and add a pan-fried sea bream fillet. Spoon over some Almond Gremolata and scatter some chopped flat-leaf parsley over the top. Serve at once.

SMOKY PRAWN
& CHICKPEA STEW

This spicy stew is deliciously warming and comforting. Seasoned with
Spanish sweet smoked paprika (*pimentón dulce*), the rich tomato sauce
envelopes the juicy seafood and chickpeas in flavour. In Spain during winter
store-cupboard staples like pulses/legumes are used alongside fresh seafood
and this surf 'n' earth dish would be typical of dishes cooked on the southern
coast. Just serve with chunks of good crusty bread for dunking.

olive oil, for frying/sautéing
½ large white onion, diced
2 garlic cloves, chopped
1 fresh red chilli/chile, deseeded
    and finely chopped
a pinch of chilli/hot red pepper
    flakes
1 teaspoon ground cumin
1 tablespoon Spanish sweet
    smoked paprika (pimentón
    dulce)
1 tablespoon tomato purée/paste
¼ teaspoon demerara/turbinado
    sugar
400-g/14-oz. can chickpeas,
    drained and rinsed
350 ml/1½ cups passata (Italian
    sieved/strained tomatoes)
12 raw large king prawns/jumbo
    shrimp, shelled with heads on
salt and freshly ground black
    pepper, to season

To serve
60 ml/¼ cup Greek yogurt
1 tablespoon freshly squeezed
    lemon juice
a small handful of flat-leaf
    parsley sprigs
extra virgin olive oil, to drizzle
crusty bread (optional)

Serves 2

Add a splash of olive oil to a large, deep frying pan/skillet and set over
a medium heat. Add the onion and fry/sauté for a few minutes until
soft and golden. Add the garlic, fresh chilli/chile and chilli/hot red
pepper flakes and cook for 1 further minute.

Stir in the cumin, paprika, tomato purée/paste and sugar, quickly
followed by the chickpeas. Pour in the passata along with a splash of
cold water and season with salt and pepper. Simmer, partially covered,
over a low heat for 15 minutes.

Put the prawns/shrimp into the pan, pushing them down slightly
into the liquid. Cook for about 4 minutes before turning them over
to continue cooking for another 2 minutes or so, until pink and
cooked through. Spoon the stew into dishes.

Whisk together the yogurt and lemon juice with 1 tablespoon of
cold water and swirl a little of it over each serving of the stew. Add
a sprig of flat-leaf parsley and a drizzle of extra virgin olive oil and
serve with good crusty bread, if you like.

FENUGREEK FISH SKILLET

Despite what is implied by its name, Fenugreek actually originates from the Middle East and is now mostly used in Indian dishes. I find that its unique flavour (slightly nutty, slightly sweet) makes a full-flavoured dish when combined with just a few simple Mediterranean ingredients. The tomato passata and honey I've used here make a rich sauce that complements the delicate flavour of white fish – I've gone with cod loins, as they are a meatier, more succulent cut than a fillet and hold together well in the sauce.

olive oil, for frying/sautéing
1 red onion, sliced
2 green (bell) peppers
3 garlic cloves, sliced
1 teaspoon ground fenugreek
3 tablespoons dried fenugreek
  leaves
500 ml/2 generous cups passata
  (Italian sieved/strained
  tomatoes)
1 tablespoon runny honey
  (preferably Greek)
4 skinless and boneless cod loin
  fillets (about 400 g/14 oz.
  total weight)
leaves from a few sprigs of fresh
  coriander/cilantro and mint,
  roughly torn
cooked rice of your choice, to
  serve (I like a mix of long grain
  and wild rice)
lime wedges, for squeezing

Serves 4

Add a splash of olive oil to a large, deep lidded frying pan/skillet and set over a medium-high heat. Fry/sauté the onion and peppers for about 10 minutes, until they have softened, then add the garlic and cook for a further 2 minutes.

Add the ground fenugreek and dried fenugreek leaves to the pan, followed by the passata and honey and pour in 125 ml/½ cup of warm water. Simmer for about 20 minutes, uncovered, until the sauce is rich and thick.

Put the cod fillets in the pan and push them down into the sauce, but not all the way – leave the surfaces just visible. Cover with the lid and leave the fish to poach in the sauce for about 6 minutes, until opaque and cooked through (how long this takes will depend on the thickness of your fillets).

Use a fish slice to remove the fillets from the pan, and spoon over the sauce. Scatter over the torn coriander/cilantro and mint leaves to garnish and serve with rice, if liked, and lime wedges for squeezing.

VILLAGE-STYLE SLOW-BAKED OCTOPUS

I remember the first time I asked my Cypriot aunt how she made this delicious dish. Her answer was 'I layer the potatoes, onions and octopus in a pot, add some red wine and bake it in the oven'. 'How long do you cook it for?' I asked, 'I put it in the oven when we leave for church and when I get home it's ready.' 'Yes, but how long do you go to church for??!' Originally cooked in a communal *fourno* (oven) in the village, everyone's pots would be popped in and collected later that day when church turned out – a foolproof method!

1.5–2-kg/3¼–4½-lb. whole fresh
   octopus
1 kg/2¼ lb. waxy potatoes
2 medium white onions
1 large, fresh, very ripe tomato
60 ml/¼ cup olive oil, to drizzle
6 garlic cloves
2 cinnamon sticks
3 dried bay leaves
1 teaspoon Greek dried oregano
a few sprigs of rosemary
freshly squeezed juice of ½
   a lemon
100 ml/scant ½ cup white wine
sea salt and freshly ground black
   pepper, to season
lemon wedges, for squeezing
   (optional)
a small handful of chopped
   flat-leaf parsley, to garnish

*a large, shallow casserole dish/
pan*

Serves 8

Preheat the oven to 180°C fan/200°C/400°F/Gas 6.

To clean the octopus, cut away the hood, just above the eyes, then cut just below the eyes and discard that piece. Turn the hood inside out and rinse, removing any sinew. Remove the 'beak' from the centre of the tentacles by just pushing it through; it'll come out quite easily. Rinse the octopus under running water and it is ready to cook.

Peel the potatoes, cut into wedges and spread over the base of a large shallow casserole dish/pan. Halve the onions and cut each half into three big chunks, and scatter these over the potatoes. Cut the tomato into 8 wedges and add these to the dish. Drizzle generously with olive oil.

Gently crack the garlic cloves, keeping the skin on and drop over the dish along with the cinnamon sticks, bay leaves, oregano and rosemary sprigs, and season with a few grinds of black pepper. Turn to mix everything together and add the lemon juice. Level everything and pour in the wine.

Place the octopus upside down (so the suckers are facing upwards) on top of the vegetables and spread out the tentacles (you can tuck the hood of the octopus under the body). Drizzle a little more olive oil over the octopus, uncovered, and put it in the preheated oven. Immediately reduce the temperature to 160°C fan/180°C/ 350°F/ Gas 4 and cook for 1½ hours, depending on how big your octopus is; check it after 1 hour by piercing the thickest part of a tentacle with a knife; it is done when it pierces easily with a tiny bit of resistance.

Remove from the oven, let rest for 10 minutes in the dish and serve warm or at room temperature. Sprinkle with chopped flat-leaf parsley and serve with lemon wedges for squeezing, if you fancy it.

AVGOLEMONO

Every culture has one recipe that is woven into the very fabric of its civilization and *avgolemono* is a dish that has been served at the kitchen table of every Greek and Cypriot ever born! This warming soul food chicken soup is laced with fresh lemon juice and egg which creates a creamy yet sharp flavour that is utterly unique. Legend says it can heal everything from a broken heart to a broken leg – I've tried it for the first ailment but opted for more modern medical practices for the second...

1.5-kg/2¼-lb. chicken
1.5–2 litres/6–8 cups water or
    chicken stock
2 dried bay leaves
4 sprigs of flat-leaf parsley
1 celery stick/stalk
200 g/1 cup Arborio/risotto rice,
    rinsed
200 g/7 oz. halloumi cheese, cut
    into 2-cm/¾-inch dice and
    brought to room temperature
3 eggs
finely grated zest and freshly
    squeezed juice of 1 lemon, plus
    extra lemon juice to taste
salt and freshly ground black
    pepper, to season
extra virgin olive oil, to drizzle
rustic bread, to serve

Serves 6

Put the chicken in a stockpot or large saucepan that is a snug fit but with some space. Add sufficient water (or stock if using) to cover the chicken by about 5 cm/2 inches and set over a medium heat. Add the bay leaves, parsley sprigs and celery stick/stalk, bring to the boil, then reduce the heat and cook at a very gentle simmer for about 1½ hours. After that time, turn off the heat, remove the chicken from the pot and set it aside on a carving plate or board and cover. Pass the stock through a sieve/strainer set over a large bowl and discard the bay leaves, parsley and celery.

Return the strained stock to the pan and set over a medium heat. Add the rice and cook for about 15–20 minutes, or until the rice is just tender, then turn off the heat. Shred a quarter of the cooked chicken and add this to the pot along with 125 ml/½ cup of cold water and the diced halloumi. (Save the remaining chicken to enjoy as leftovers.)

In a large mixing bowl, beat the eggs with the lemon juice, then push a ladle into the soup avoiding any rice, chicken or halloumi and, very slowly, pour the ladleful of soup into the beaten eggs, continuously whisking with a balloon whisk as you do, add 2 ladlefuls in total. The aim is to temper the egg mixture to bring the temperature up without cooking it. If you pour the liquid in too quickly, you'll cook the eggs and it will curdle. Once the eggs are tempered slowly pour the mixture back into the stockpot, stirring as you do. Taste the soup, add more lemon juice and a little salt to taste.

If the soup needs warming, put it back over a low heat for a few minutes, stirring continuously, but don't let it simmer or it will curdle. Once warmed through, ladle the soup into bowls, ensuring everyone gets chicken, rice and halloumi, then top each one up with more soup. Finish each bowl with a few grinds of black pepper, a pinch of salt, a drizzle of extra virgin olive oil, and a pinch of lemon zest.

ROASTED RACK OF PORK
WITH PEACH, ROSÉ & ROSEMARY GLAZE

At Greek Easter it's not uncommon to cook a whole goat or pig to celebrate the end of Lent and fasting, meat having traditionally been more of a luxury reserved for a celebratory meal than an everyday food. This recipe indulges that idea with a slow-roasted rack of pork, smothered in a peach and rosemary glaze that's been enriched with rosé wine. Quite simply, it's delicious! As a rack of pork is a lean meat, despite the blanket of fat, so overcooking it can make it tough. To avoid this, I brine the meat for a few hours before cooking to ensure a succulent and mouth-watering roast.

2–2.5-kg/5¼–5½-lb. pork rack, French trimmed, skinned, fat left on
250 g/1 heaping cup salt
200 g/1 cup white sugar, for brining (plus 1–2 teaspoons extra, to taste)
1 whole garlic bulb (about 10–12 cloves)
6 sprigs of fresh rosemary
6 dried bay leaves
1 tablespoon olive oil
6 ripe peaches, stoned/pitted and chopped
250 ml/1 cup rosé or white wine
1 white onion, thickly sliced
a knob/pat of butter
salt and freshly ground black pepper, to season
a simple green salad and fried potatoes, to serve

Serves 6–8

Making the brine couldn't be easier. Find a large non-reactive container (plastic, glass or stainless steel) big enough to take the whole rack of pork. Put the salt and 200 g/1 cup of sugar in the container with about 1 litre/4 cups of cold water and stir until fully dissolved. Add a few of the rosemary sprigs, about 6 garlic cloves, lightly cracked (you can leave the skin on) and the bay leaves. Submerge the whole rack of pork in the brine. Cover and keep in the fridge for a few hours. (If you can't fit it in your fridge, add ice cubes to the water to keep it chilled, or you can even put it outside if it's a cold day.) You will need to remove the pork from the brine 30 minutes before you plan to cook it, to dry it and bring it to room temperature.

Whilst the pork is in the brine, make the peach glaze. Crush 2 garlic cloves and add to a small saucepan with the olive oil. Set over a low heat and just warm the garlic through (without letting it colour), then add the leaves stripped from half a rosemary sprig followed by the peaches, wine (reserving a splash to deglaze the roasting pan later) and 1 teaspoon of sugar. Season with salt and pepper and simmer for 15 minutes over a low heat, uncovered, or until the peaches have broken down but still retain a little texture. Taste, as depending on the sweetness of your peaches and wine, you may want to add a little more sugar. Remove from the heat, siphon off one third of the mixture and reserve for the sauce.

Preheat the oven to 200°C fan/220°C/425°F/Gas 7.

Scatter the onion slices, any remaining garlic cloves (lightly cracked with the skin on) and a few sprigs of rosemary into a large roasting pan and place the pork on top. Score the fat on the pork with a small sharp knife, without piercing the flesh, and season with salt and pepper. Spoon over two-thirds of the peach glaze.

Roast the pork in the preheated oven for 1½ hours, then remove from the oven, transfer to a tray and loosely cover with kitchen foil. Let rest for 30 minutes (this resting period is important as it ensures the meat finishes cooking internally and is tender).

Set the roasting pan and its contents over a low heat and add the reserved splash of wine. Heat, scraping off any of the burnt bits, and simmer for 5 minutes, until the wine has reduced by half. Remove from the heat, add the butter and the remaining peach glaze and whisk it in until emulsified. Pass through a sieve/strainer into a sauce jug/pitcher. Put the rested pork rack on a large wooden board ready to be carved and serve with the jug/pitcher of warmed peach glaze on the side for pouring. The perfect accompaniments to this are a simple green salad and crisply fried potatoes sprinkled with a little Greek dried oregano.

BRAISED CELERY LOUVI

Louvi is a traditional Cypriot dish that is a regular staple in most homes.
It consists of small, creamy black-eyed beans/peas, cooked down with
locally foraged *horta* (Greek wild greens) and these can be anything from
dandelions to chard – see my recipe for Garlic Horta on page 122. Here,
I've used celery instead of the greens as it takes on its own unique flavour
and texture when slowly braised and makes a delicious change.

400-g/14-oz. can black-eyed
  beans/peas, drained and rinsed
  or 115 g/heaping ½ cup dried
  (250 g/1 cup cooked weight),
  see Note, below right
1 celery head
olive oil, for frying/sautéing
1 medium white onion, sliced
1 fresh tomato, diced
250 ml/1 cup vegetable stock
8 Kalamata olives, stoned/pitted
  and halved
2 tablespoons extra virgin
  olive oil
freshly squeezed juice of
  ½ a lemon
a handful of flat-leaf parsley
  leaves, coarsely chopped
salt and freshly ground black
  pepper

Serves 6

Top and tail the celery head and cut the sticks/stalks it into 7.5-cm/ 3-inch lengths, reserving the fronds to garnish.

Add a splash of olive oil to a saucepan and set over a medium heat. Add the onion and fry/sauté it for a few minutes until it starts to turn translucent but not brown, then add the celery and cook, uncovered, for a few more minutes.

Add the tomato, season generously with salt and pepper, then add the stock, cover the pan with a lid or plate, reduce the heat and leave it to simmer for about 30 minutes, or until the celery softens but is not mushy (check it every so often).

Once the celery is cooked, remove the lid, add the olives to the pan, along with the cooked beans, and simmer for a few more minutes to reduce the cooking liquid until there is a thin layer left in the pan, then remove from the heat.

Fold in the extra virgin olive oil, lemon juice and chopped flat-leaf parsley and season generously with salt and pepper.

Transfer to a serving dish, chop the reserved celery fronds and scatter them over the top to garnish.

Note: I often use canned beans of all varieties in my recipes for convenience, but you can cook dried black-eyed beans/peas from scratch without soaking them first, which makes it a more attractive proposition here! Simply rinse, add to a pan with three times their volume in water and a squeeze of lemon juice to help them keep their colour. Simmer gently for 1½ hours, or until soft, and use as directed in the recipe above.

RABBIT PEPITORIA

Pollo en Pepitoria is a traditional Spanish recipe made with older hens, which for most small, self-sufficient communities in the Mediterranean was much more sustainable than cooking a young chicken. In recent generations chickens are used that take less time to cook and are much more tender. *Pepitoria* gets its distinctive taste from simple ingredients and those local to the region; hard-boiled/cooked egg yolks, stale bread, toasted almonds and saffron. These are all ground together to create a paste known as *majado* which is used to thicken the cooking juices. Farmed rabbit is widely used throughout the Mediterranean as a local and sustainable meat and works perfectly in this recipe. If you can't get farmed rabbit (or you would prefer it) you can use a jointed chicken instead.

15 whole blanched almonds

a pinch of saffron threads

1 small slice of stale white bread, cubed or torn

2 eggs, hard-boiled/cooked

a 1.5-kg/3¼-lb. farmed rabbit, jointed (or a 1.5-kg/3¼-lb. chicken, jointed)

olive oil, for frying/sautéing

1 medium white onion, diced

2 slices Serrano ham, torn

2 garlic cloves, diced

60 ml/¼ cup Spanish sweet sherry, plus 1 extra tablespoon

125 ml/½ cup white wine

200 ml/generous ¾ cup chicken stock

salt and freshly ground black pepper, to season

a handful of flat-leaf parsley leaves, finely chopped

toasted flaked/slivered almonds, to garnish

white rice or fried potatoes, to serve (optional)

a pestle and mortar (optional)

Serves 4

First make the majado paste. Put the almonds in a small dry frying pan/skillet set over a low heat and lightly toast; do not let them burn. Remove the pan from the heat and immediately drop in the saffron, then tip the contents into a pestle and mortar or small food processor. Add the bread and peel the eggs and add the egg yolks (reserving the egg whites). Pulverize it all until you have a smooth paste. Set aside.

Line a plate with paper towels. Season the rabbit with salt and pepper. Add a splash of olive oil to a lidded frying pan/skillet and set it over a medium heat. Fry/sauté the rabbit until golden, in batches if necessary, transferring the rabbit from the pan to the lined plate.

Drain away any excess fat from the pan (especially if using chicken) and reintroduce 1 tablespoon of it back into the pan. Fry/sauté the onion over a low heat, until translucent, then add the ham and once crispy, stir in the garlic. Pour in the sherry and white wine and simmer until reduced by half, scraping off any of the burnt bits in the pan as you go. Whisk in the majado and once combined pour in the stock, reintroduce the rabbit and season with salt and pepper.

Partially cover the pan with a lid and leave to simmer gently for about 30 minutes, or until the rabbit is cooked through; remove the lid towards the end of cooking if you want the sauce to thicken. About 5 minutes before you finish cooking, fold in the extra sherry or omit if you prefer a milder flavour. Leave to sit in the pan for 5 minutes before garnishing with toasted almonds, flat-leaf parsley and finely diced reserved egg whites. Serve with white rice or fried potatoes.

OXTAIL OSSO BUCO
WITH SOURED BULGUR WHEAT

Osso buco translates as 'bone with hole' and this luxurious Italian dish is usually made with veal, but I like to slow cook oxtail to create an equally lip-smacking and glossy sauce to rival it. *Trahana* is a filling, porridgy soup eaten in Cyprus and Greece, made from kibbled wheat and fermented goats' or sheeps' milk. I've taken my inspiration from this dish to create a soft, bulgur wheat which gets its sharp, tangy taste from the yogurt. Its unique flavour and texture make it the perfect backdrop to the rich osso buco juices.

a splash of vegetable oil
1.5 kg/3¼ lb. oxtail, fat trimmed
olive oil, for frying/sautéing
2 celery sticks/stalks, finely diced
1 large carrot, finely diced
1 medium white onion, diced
2 garlic cloves, chopped
1 tablespoon finely chopped
    dried porcini mushrooms
3 dried bay leaves
4 dates, pitted and sliced
2 heaped tablespoons plain/
    all-purpose flour
500 ml/2 cups white wine
500 ml/2 cups chicken stock
salt and freshly ground black
    pepper, to season
1 quantity of Almond Gremolata
    (see page 100), to serve

For the Soured Bulgur Wheat
150 g/1 scant cup coarse bulgur
1 vegetable bouillon cube
½ teaspoon salt
60 ml/¼ cup Greek yogurt
50 ml/3½ tablespoons extra
    virgin olive oil
freshly squeezed lemon juice,
    to taste
a handful of chopped flat-leaf
    parsley leaves, to garnish

Serves 6

Preheat the oven to 170°C fan/190°C/375°F/Gas 5.

Season the oxtail with salt and pepper. Add the vegetable oil to a lidded, flameproof casserole dish/pan (this needs to be snug-fitting to ensure that the oxtail is full submerged in liquid when it goes in the oven) and set over a medium heat. Add the oxtail, brown the meat for about 6 minutes and once all the meat is done, pour away the oil.

Heat a little olive oil over medium heat in the same dish/pan and add the celery, carrot and onion. Fry/sauté until softened, then add the garlic and mushrooms and cook for 1 minute further. Return the oxtail to the dish, along with any meat juices, and add the bay leaves, dates and flour. Fry/sauté this mixture for 2 minutes, stirring, then pour in the wine. Bring to a boil, then reduce to a simmer to cook off the alcohol. Once the liquid has reduced by a third, pour in the stock, cover the dish/pan tightly with its lid and cook in the preheated oven for 3 hours. Remove from the oven and let rest with the lid on for 30 minutes before serving.

While it is resting, make the Soured Bulgur Wheat. Put the bulgur in a large saucepan, crumble in the bouillon cube and add 750 ml/ 3 cups of cold water and the salt. Set over a medium heat and bring to the boil, whisking continuously, then reduce the heat so bubbles barely break the surface. Simmer for 20 minutes, stirring vigorously every 5 minutes (adding a splash more water if it starts to dry out).

While the bulgur is still a bit sloppy, turn off the heat, wait for it to stop bubbling, then stir in the yogurt and extra virgin olive oil, season to taste with salt and pepper and lemon juice.

Serve immediately, with the osso bucco on top and garnished with a sprinkle of chopped flat-leaf parsley. Offer a dish of the tangy Almond Gremolata on the side for spooning.

PLENTY
SALADS & SIDES

GARLIC HORTA

Horta vrasa translates as boiled wild greens. If you can get wild garlic or dandelion leaves by all means include them, as this recipe is about using any edible, foraged wild green. My recipe includes a good dose of warm, garlic-infused extra virgin olive oil for a little extra goodness and punch of flavour.

250 ml/1 cup extra virgin olive oil
2 garlic cloves, thickly sliced
500 g/18 oz. any young leafy
   greens, such as collard, kale,
   spring greens and/or cabbage
400 g/14 oz. rainbow Swiss
   chard
250 g/9 oz. white chicory/
   Belgian endive (witloof)
a large handful of flat-leaf parsley
   sprigs
freshly squeezed juice of 1 lemon
salt and freshly ground black
   pepper, to season

Serves 6

Put about 60 ml/⅓ cup of the oil into a saucepan along with the sliced garlic and set over a low heat. Warm through, just enough to help the garlic flavour the oil, don't cook it. Remove from the heat, pour in the remaining oil and set aside.

Cut away any very thick stalks from the young greens or Swiss chard, otherwise leave them whole. Trim the root from the chicory/Belgian endive and quarter lengthways.

Bring a large saucepan of salted water to the boil and drop in the young greens and chard and simmer for about 8 minutes, or until the stalks are soft but not mushy (any thick stalks you have removed from the leaves can go in a couple of minutes earlier). Remove with a slotted spoon and transfer to a colander to steam dry. Add the whole sprigs of flat-leaf parsley and chicory to the same water and simmer for about 3 minutes before removing.

Put all the cooked greens into a serving bowl, fold in the garlic-infused oil and lemon juice and season with salt and pepper.

TENDERSTEM BROCCOLI
& ASPARAGUS
WITH GARLIC & CHILLI

There is always beauty to be found in simplicity. This green side dish
goes with just about everything. I sauté the broccoli and asparagus which
enhances their flavour and also means they hold their shape. The technique
of adding a splash of water to the pan to finish cooking them with steam is
one I use a lot and it works with most vegetables that require quick cooking;
adding the garlic and chilli/chile is just my preference...

olive oil, for frying/sautéing
200 g/7 oz. Tenderstem
  broccoli/broccolini
200 g/7 oz. fresh asparagus,
  trimmed
½ red fresh red chilli/chile,
  deseeded and finely sliced
2 garlic cloves, thickly sliced
1 teaspoon freshly squeezed
  lemon juice
a small knob/pat of butter
toasted flaked/slivered almonds,
  to garnish
finely grated lemon zest, to
  sprinkle (optional)
salt and freshly ground black
  pepper

Serves 4

Heat a frying pan/skillet until smoking hot and add a splash of olive
oil, immediately followed by the broccoli. Fry/sauté for a few minutes
before adding the asparagus, then season with salt and pepper.

Continue to cook over a high heat for another 2 minutes or so, then
stir through the garlic and chilli/chile and immediately follow with
2 tablespoons of cold water. (This instantly creates steam to cook
through the vegetables and stops the garlic and chilli/chile catching
and burning.)

Cook until the liquid has evaporated, then remove the pan from
the heat, squeeze in a little lemon juice (no more than 1 teaspoon),
add the butter and allow it to melt and coat the vegetables. Garnish
with a scattering of almond flakes/slivers and serve. Feel free to
sprinkle over some finely grated lemon zest to add a little more colour,
if you fancy it.

PARMESAN POLENTA

This creamy polenta makes the perfect accompaniment to a variety of dishes, especially those with a little sauce looking for something to mingle with. It's delicious served with my Rich Mushroom Ragù on page 93.

200 g/1⅓ cups coarse yellow polenta/cornmeal
½ teaspoon salt
a knob/pat of butter or a splash of olive oil, as preferred
3 tablespoons finely grated Parmesan cheese
250 ml/1 cup whole milk (or single/light cream if you want it very rich)
salt and freshly ground black pepper, to season

Serves 6

Put 1.25 litres/5 cups of cold water in a large saucepan and add the polenta, the salt and a few grinds of black pepper. Set over a medium heat and bring to the boil, whisking continuously. Once the water starts to boil, reduce the heat to low and continue to cook at a very gentle simmer, stirring every 5 minutes, to stop it catching.

After about 40 minutes taste the polenta, you want it to be soft and molten but with a little texture, so it can take up to 45 minutes to reach that stage. Once cooked, remove from the heat, beat in the butter and Parmesan cheese with a wooden spoon, until melted. Add the milk a little at a time and beat in until it is all incorporated and the polenta is loose in texture and creamy. Season to taste with salt and pepper and let rest in the pan until you are ready to serve it.

POMMES ALIGOT

This French dish of cheesey whipped potatoes is often served with sausages, but works well with veggies too, try it with the Sicilian Caponata on page 63.

1 kg/2¼ lb. floury potatoes, unpeeled
400 ml/scant 1¾ cups whole milk, warmed
40 g/3 tablespoons butter
50 ml/3½ tablespoons olive oil
2 garlic cloves, crushed
150 g/5½ oz. Gruyère cheese, grated
150 g/5½ oz. firm Mozzarella cheese, grated
salt and freshly ground black pepper

Serves 6

Bring a large saucepan of salted water to the boil and add the potatoes. Boil them for 20–30 minutes, until cooked through (this will depend on their size). Once a knife or skewer passes through a potato easily, drain them and leave uncovered to steam dry. When they are cool enough to handle, remove the skins (rubbing them away with paper towels usually works) then mash by hand and push through a coarse sieve/strainer with the back of a spoon.

Put the mashed potatoes into a large saucepan and set over low heat. Add the warm milk, butter, olive oil, garlic and half the grated cheeses. Beat with a wooden spoon until the cheese has melted and is fully incorporated, then beat in the remaining cheese, again until melted. It will pull away from the sides of the saucepan when it is ready. Serve warm as a side dish.

SPICED LABNEH

Labneh is a fresh soft cheese that is so versatile and simple to make at home as you are just separating the whey from the yogurt. Once the *labneh* is made you can fold in any flavourings you like: dried or fresh herbs, crushed garlic, fresh or dried chilli/hot pepper, whatever takes your fancy. For me a drizzle of olive oil and the crushed spices I've used here hit the spot and it's delicious served with my Socca with Charred Asparagus recipe on page 10. Unusually, I don't recommend a set Greek yogurt for this recipe – a runnier natural/plain yogurt works best as I tend to find anything thicker creates a very stiff cream cheese and I prefer a softer texture. I've been generous with the spice mixture so store any leftover in an airtight jar and use it as a seasoning.

600 g/3 cups natural/plain
    yogurt (not Greek-style)
1 teaspoon salt
1 tablespoon freshly squeezed
    lemon juice
60 ml/¼ cup olive oil

For the Toasted Spice Mix
1 teaspoon cumin seeds
½ teaspoon fennel seeds
½ teaspoon coriander seeds
6 pink peppercorns
a pinch of salt
a small pinch of ground chilli/
    chili powder

Serves 4

To make the Toasted Spice Mix, toast all the spices in a dry frying pan/skillet for 1 minute; don't let them burn. Tip them into a mortar and grind to a powder with a pestle. Store in an airtight jar until needed.

To make the labneh, mix the yogurt, salt and lemon juice together in a bowl. Set a sieve/strainer over a separate bowl and line it with a clean tea towel/dish cloth. Spoon in the yogurt mixture, bring the overhanging cloth together at the top and twist it a few times to create a tight ball of yogurt below; you should see a little moisture starting to come through immediately. Give it a few turns to give it some pressure. Transfer to the fridge to sit for at least 12–48 hours; the longer you leave it, the thicker your labneh will be.

Before removing the labneh from the towel/cloth, squeeze it a little just to remove any excess liquid then tip it out into a bowl. It can be used in your recipe straightaway or, as is traditional, you can roll it into balls and store them in a jar submerged in olive oil; it will keep in the fridge for up to 2 weeks. I sometimes roll a few of the labneh balls in the Toasted Spice Mix and serve them drizzled with a little honey and toast for a quick snack.

YIAYIA'S HERB SALAD
WITH FETA DRESSING

A simple salad with aromatic herbs, crisp white cabbage, peppery rocket/
arugula and more, all woven together and dressed with a molten feta
vinaigrette. Traditionally in Cyprus this would be concocted with whatever
local herbs and greens were growing in the village and a local cheese.

½ romaine/Cos lettuce, shredded
⅕ white cabbage, shredded
¼ green (bell) pepper, deseeded
   and thinly sliced
a few large handfuls of rocket/
   arugula
fronds from a handful of dill
leaves from a handful of flat-leaf
   parsley
leaves from a handful of
   coriander/cilantro
leaves from a handful of mint
12 large basil leaves, torn
½ cucumber, halved lengthways,
   cut into thin bite-size wedges
100 g/3½ oz. sweet, ripe vine
   tomatoes, cut into small
   chunks
½ small red onion, thinly sliced
100 g/1 cup Kalamata olives,
   halved and stoned/pitted

For the Feta Dressing
50 g/2 oz. feta cheese
60 ml/⅓ cup extra virgin olive oil
60 ml/⅓ cup red wine vinegar
1 tablespoon Greek dried
   oregano
a squeeze of fresh lemon juice
freshly ground black pepper,
   to season

Serves 6

Prep all the salad ingredients and put them in a large mixing bowl.

To make the dressing, mash the feta with the back of a fork and
put it in a screw-top jar, along with the rest of the dressing ingredients.
Tighten the lid and give it a good shake to emulsify, add a drop of
water if it needs loosening. Taste and add a few grinds of pepper to
taste – it will be punchy but you want it that way!

Just before you are ready to serve, give the jar another gentle
shake and pour the dressing over the salad. Toss to ensure the salad
ingredients are all coated.

Transfer to a salad bowl, leaving any excess dressing behind, and
serve immediately.

GRIDDLED GEM LETTUCE
WITH PANGRITATA

Pangritata is a fancy word for flavoured breadcrumbs, literally 'grated bread', and once fried in lashings of olive oil with a few herbs and garlic added they make a flavoursome crispy topping to a host of dishes, from pasta to salads. In this instance their perfect texture is a great accent to my griddled gem lettuce which I enjoy cooking outside on the barbecue, but inside on a cast-iron griddle pan or heavy skillet is fine too if the weather is hostile.

2 Little Gem lettuces/baby Cos
   or romaine
3 tablespoons olive oil
1 garlic clove, thickly sliced
a small handful of flat-leaf
   parsley
125 ml/½ cup chicken or
   vegetable stock
1 tablespoon butter
a squeeze of fresh lemon juice
salt and freshly ground black
   pepper, to season

For the Pangritata
2 tablespoons olive oil
1 garlic clove, thickly sliced
100 g/2 cups fresh breadcrumbs
   made with day-old bread (see
   Note, below)
leaves picked from 2 sprigs of
   thyme
a pinch of dried chilli/hot red
   pepper flakes
salt and freshly ground black
   pepper, to season

Serves 4

To make the Pangritata, pour the oil into a small frying pan/skillet and add the garlic. Set over a low heat and once the garlic starts to sizzle increase the heat to medium and drop in the breadcrumbs and thyme, fry/sauté until crisp and golden then remove from the pan onto a plate lined with paper towels. Season with salt and pepper and fold in the dried chilli/hot red pepper flakes.

Trim the lettuce by cutting off the very end of the stalk and removing any loose leaves. Halve each lettuce lengthways, drizzle olive oil over the cut side and season with salt and pepper.

Take a heavy frying pan/skillet/cast iron griddle pan that just fits the lettuce halves in one layer, but they are nice and snug. Set the pan over a high heat and when smoking hot, put the lettuce halves cut-side down in and sear for about 3 minutes, or until the leaves are charred. Drop in the garlic and parsley and immediately turn over the lettuce and pour in the stock and simmer, uncovered, until the liquid reduces by half. Turn off the heat, drop the butter, add a little squeeze of lemon juice and swirl it around the pan to combine.

Put the lettuce halves on a serving dish, spoon over the pan juices and finish with a sprinkle of the pangritata just before serving to keep it nice and crisp.

Note: The best way to make fresh breadcrumbs is to use the end pieces from a sliced loaf, wholemeal or white. Simply tear into smaller pieces and put in the bowl of food processor and process to obtain crumbs. They freeze well, so make a batch rather than throw bread away, and keep them for when you need them.

ROASTED RADICCHIO
WITH BLUE CHEESE DRESSING

Radicchio has a striking red and white colour and natural bitterness that, when roasted, mellows to a warm smokiness. A tangy blue cheese dressing with crunchy walnuts and seeds is all it needs, oh and a little drizzle of sticky pomegranate molasses...

100 g/½ cup pearled spelt
2 medium radicchio heads
a splash of olive oil
2 tablespoons butter, melted
1 tablespoon runny honey
4 walnuts halves, crumbled
1 tablespoon toasted pumpkin
   seeds/pepitas
2 tablespoons pomegranate
   molasses
salt and freshly ground black
   pepper, to season

For the Blue Cheese Dressing
50 g/2 oz. any blue cheese
3 tablespoons Greek yogurt
2 tablespoons extra virgin
   olive oil
a few squeezes of fresh lemon
   juice
a pinch of finely chopped
   flat-leaf parsley
a pinch of salt

Serves 4–6

Preheat the oven to 200°C fan/220°C/425°F/Gas 7.

Rinse the pearled spelt under running water. Tip into a large saucepan and cover with salted water. Simmer for about 20–30 minutes, or until cooked; it should be chewy but without any crunch. Drain, season and set aside.

Trim the radicchio and quarter lengthways (or cut into sixths if they are on the large side) and put them on a baking sheet. Drizzle with a little olive oil, the melted butter and just a smidge of honey and season with salt and pepper. Toss with your hands to coat evenly. Roast in the preheated oven for about 15–20 minutes, turning them once during cooking. They are done when the stalk is just knife tender. Pour the cooked spelt into the baking sheet to coat in any of the juices, then transfer everything to a serving dish or platter.

To make the Blue Cheese Dressing, simply mash all the ingredients together with a fork in a small bowl and add a splash of water if it needs loosening to a pouring consistency. Drizzle the dressing over the radicchio and spelt, sprinkle with crumbled walnuts and pumpkin seeds and finish with a drizzle with pomegranate molasses

TOMATO PANZANELLA

Leftover bread features often in a Mediterranean diet, continuing that philosophy of nothing going to waste, including bread that is past its best. This classic Italian salad of beautiful ripe tomatoes, their juices plumping up stale bread with drizzle of golden olive oil, and splash of sharp vinegar is a meal in its own right. A ball of fresh mozzarella ripped over the salad is totally optional and acceptable!

500 g/18 oz. ripe heirloom/
   heritage tomatoes (use a
   variety of different colours)
400 g/14 oz. day-old rustic bread
¼ small red onion, very thinly
   sliced
leaves from 1 sprig of basil, torn
leaves from 2 sprigs of flat-leaf
   parsley, torn
6 tablespoons extra virgin
   olive oil
3 tablespoons white wine vinegar
1 small garlic clove, crushed
a pinch of dried oregano
   (preferably Greek)
sea salt flakes and freshly ground
   black pepper

Serves 4

Cut all the tomatoes into bite-size chunks and put them in a mixing bowl, scraping any juice into it as well. Sprinkle over a generous pinch or two of salt flakes and add a few grinds of black pepper (coarse, cracked pepper works well here).

Tear or slice the bread into pieces similar in size to your tomato chunks and put these in the bowl with the tomatoes, folding them through all the lovely juices to moisten. Scatter the onion, basil and flat-leaf parsley over the top.

Lightly whisk together the olive oil and vinegar in a small bowl until emulsified and stir in the garlic and oregano. Pour over the salad, fold everything together, cover and leave at room temperature for 30 minutes, then serve.

POTATOES WITH DILL & GARLIC

I was first introduced to these by my Bulgarian sister-in-law's parents one Christmas. I couldn't stop eating them! Dried dill is the secret here.

2 tablespoons butter
5 garlic cloves, chopped
60 ml/¼ cup olive oil
1 kg/2¼ lb. small potatoes (floury, not waxy salad ones)
1 tablespoon dried dill (preferably Bulgarian or Greek)
a few sprigs of dill, to garnish
salt, to season

Serves 6

Preheat the oven to 180°C fan/200°C/400°F/Gas 6.

Beat together the butter, garlic and olive oil in a large bowl and set aside.

Peel the potatoes and cut them into 2.5-cm/1-inch chunks. Add these to the bowl and toss to ensure all the potatoes are coated in the butter mixture. Arrange them in a single layer on a baking sheet and scatter over the dried dill, turning them to dust evenly.

Roast in the preheated oven for 45–60 minutes, until cooked through. Transfer to a serving bowl, season generously with salt and garnish with the fresh dill sprigs.

FRENCH POTATO SALAD

This divine, garlicky, herby potato salad is reminiscent of many I've enjoyed in France. They all rely on good olive oil, garlic, and here, also Dijon mustard.

500 g/18 oz. waxy new potatoes
500 g/18 oz. red new potatoes
a large knob/pat of butter
2 garlic cloves, crushed
6 spring onions/scallions, sliced
a small handful each of dill and flat-leaf parsley, torn

For the vinaigrette
50 ml/3½ tablespoons extra virgin olive oil
2½ tablespoons white wine vinegar
1 tablespoon Dijon mustard
salt and freshly ground black pepper

Serves 6

Make the vinaigrette by whisking together the oil, vinegar and Dijon mustard until emulsified and season with salt and pepper. Set aside.

Slice the potatoes in half lengthways or quarter them if they are on the large side. Boil in a saucepan of salted water for 10–15 minutes, until tender. Once cooked, drain and leave in a sieve/strainer to rest. Add the butter to the saucepan the potatoes were cooked in, and stir in the garlic; the residual heat of the pan will melt the butter.

Once the butter is melted tip the potatoes back into the pan. Run a knife through them a few times to break them up a little and help them absorb some of that lovely garlicky butter. Season with salt and pepper and add the spring onions/scallions, half the herbs and the dressing. Fold everything together to ensure it is all coated.

Leave to rest for a few minutes before tipping into a serving dish and finish by scattering the remaining herbs over the top.

DELIGHT
SWEET TREATS

FLOURLESS ALMOND & ORANGE CAKE

Oh for oranges and almonds… sigh. This cake is my wife's favourite, despite being flourless it remains moist and the puréed whole oranges give it a sharp vibrancy that is hard to beat. I've dressed this up by decorating it, but if I'm honest, most of the time in our house it barely makes it out of the baking pan before we're cutting away slices each time we walk past.

4 oranges
400 g/4 cups ground almonds
1½ teaspoons baking powder
400 g/2 cups caster/superfine or granulated sugar
finely grated zest and freshly squeezed juice of ½ a lemon
12 UK small/US medium eggs

For the glaze and decoration
6 tablespoons apricot conserve
1 tablespoon brandy (preferably Greek)
250 ml/1 cup Greek yogurt
1 tablespoon caster/superfine sugar
grated zest of ½ an orange and ½ a lemon
½–1 orange, peeled and separated into segments
1 tablespoon coarsely chopped pistachio kernels
icing/confectioners' sugar, to dust (optional)

a 22-cm/8½-inch diameter springform cake pan, lightly greased with butter

Serves 8

Bring a large saucepan of water to the boil, add the oranges whole and boil them for 2 hours, topping up the water as necessary to keep them fully submerged.

Once soft, gently lift the oranges out of the water and let cool for 10 minutes before putting in a blender. Pulse until they are a pulp and then pass this through a fine sieve/strainer set over a bowl, pushing it through with the back of a spoon. Set aside.

Preheat the oven to 180°C fan/200°C/400°F/Gas 6.

Combine the ground almonds, baking powder and caster/granulated sugar in a large mixing bowl. Stir in the sieved/strained orange pulp, add a small squeeze of lemon juice and mix to combine. Whisk the eggs and pass through a coarse sieve/strainer directly into the bowl and beat until fully incorporated.

Pour the mixture into the prepared cake pan. Bake in the preheated oven for 30 minutes, then remove and let cool in the pan.

To make the glaze, put the apricot conserve in a small bowl with the brandy, add 1 tablespoon cold water and stir to combine. Brush this glaze over the cooled cake to give it a little shine.

Put the yogurt and caster/superfine sugar in a bowl and stir to dissolve the sugar. Decorate the cake by spooning the sweetened yogurt over the cake, arrange the orange segments on top and finish with the pistachios and a sprinkle of orange and lemon zest. Adding a dusting of icing/confectioners' sugar is optional.

CAROB CREAM CHEESE ESPRESSO CUPS

Carob trees are found throughout the Mediterranean and Middle East, and their dark brown pods have a unique naturally sweet taste, which is similar to chocolate but less bitter and with caramel notes. Thick, syrupy carob molasses is becoming more and more popular as an ingredient and I've paired it in this recipe with espresso coffee, all folded into a creamy base to create a deliciously easy no-cook dessert.

1 tablespoon butter

2 digestive biscuits/graham crackers, crushed into crumbs

a pinch of sugar

a pinch of salt

225 g/1 cup ricotta cheese

125 g/heaping ½ cup mascarpone cheese

2 tablespoons icing/confectioners' sugar

3 tablespoons carob molasses

1 tablespoon strong freshly made espresso coffee

1 tablespoon brandy, preferably Greek (optional)

about 6–8 whole blanched hazelnuts, halved

a disposable piping/pastry bag (optional)

4 espresso cups, or similar size dessert pots

Makes 4

Put the butter in a small saucepan and set over a low heat to melt (or alternatively melt in the microwave). When melted add the biscuit/cookie crumbs and mix in, along with the sugar and salt.

Meanwhile, put the rest of the ingredients, except the hazelnuts, in a large bowl and use an electric hand-held whisk or a balloon whisk to beat together until you have a silky-smooth mixture. Taste it and add more molasses, coffee or brandy to taste, then cover and put it in the fridge for 15 minutes.

Put the hazelnuts in a small, dry frying pan/skillet and toast over low heat until lightly golden, taking care not to let them burn. Tip them out of the pan and set aside to cool.

Put the carob cream cheese mixture into a piping/pastry bag (if using), snip the end off with scissors and pipe the mixture in circles to fill each cup. (Alternatively spoon the mixture into the cups and level the surface of each one with the back of a spoon.)

Top each cup with a few toasted hazelnut halves, then crush the remaining nuts and sprinkle these over the top to finish. Keep covered in the fridge until you are ready to serve.

NECTARINE & FENNEL GALETTE

This free-form galette is for those who enjoy the beauty found in imperfection; a piece of pastry just rolled out flat and piled high with seasonal fruit, its edges roughly folded over to form a crust and then baked to perfection in whatever shape it happens to form. For me, the combination of slightly sweet nectarines sprinkled with fennel seeds is unusual and delicious and the perfect ending to any summer meal.

70 g/generous ⅓ cup demerara/
    turbinado sugar
2 tablespoons cornflour/
    cornstarch
5 ripe nectarines, cut into
    2.5-cm/1-inch segments
about 350 g/¾ lb. ready-made
    shortcrust pastry dough,
    chilled
a generous pinch of semolina
2–3 teaspoons fennel seeds,
    lightly toasted
1 tablespoon butter
1 egg, beaten
1 tablespoon apricot preserve
1 teaspoon lemon juice
a small pinch of sea salt flakes
vanilla ice cream, to serve
    (optional)

a large baking sheet

baking parchment

Serves 8

Preheat the oven to 200°C fan/220°C/425°F/Gas 7.

Put the sugar and cornflour/cornstarch in a large bowl and mix together. Add the nectarine segments and toss them in the mixture to dust.

Put the pastry onto a large sheet of parchment paper and roll it out to a rectangle of about 30 x 38 cm/12 x 15 inches and 3 mm/⅛ inch thick. Sprinkle the semolina over the pastry, focusing on the centre, then pile the nectarines evenly along the middle, leaving a 5-cm/2-inch lip around the edge. Spoon over any remaining sugar and cornflour/cornstarch, scatter the fennel seeds over the top and dot roughly half the butter over the nectarines. Lift the edges of the pastry up around the fruit, using your fingers to roll and pinch it to create a free-form crust. Brush the beaten egg over the crust to glaze.

Lift the galette into a baking sheet and put in the preheated oven. Immediately reduce the heat to 180°C fan/200°C/400°F/Gas 6. Bake for 40 minutes, or until the fruit is cooked and the pastry golden.

Remove from the oven, transfer to a wire rack whilst still on the baking parchment and leave to cool. Once cooled, melt the remaining butter (I pop it into the microwave for 10 seconds) and mix it with the apricot preserve and lemon juice in a small bowl. Brush this over the fruit to give it a nice sheen and dust with a small pinch of sea salt flakes. Serve with a decent vanilla ice cream, if you fancy it.

BAKED PEARS
WITH LEMON-SCENTED GERANIUM

The lemon-scented geranium my mum grows in pots in her garden only takes the slightest brush when walking past it to release a heady citrus perfume into the air. These beautiful plants are safe to eat and here they lend their delicate aroma to my baked pears. The fruit is cooked in wine which reduces along with the pear juices to create a balanced, bittersweet syrup. Most varieties of pear bake well, but avoid comice, as their tender flesh tends to fall apart when baked whole. If you can't source lemon-scented geranium, you can use sprigs of lemon verbena instead.

6 large fresh pears
a squeeze of lemon juice
350 ml/1½ cups rosé wine
100 g/½ cup demerara/turbinado sugar
3 tablespoons runny honey
40 g/½ cup flaked/slivered almonds
100 g/7 tablespoons salted butter
a few pinches of ground cinnamon
leaves from 3 lemon-scented geranium sprigs, washed

For the Chantilly Cream
300 ml/1¼ cups double/heavy cream
3 tablespoons icing/confectioners' sugar
a few drops of vanilla extract

a high-sided baking sheet

Serves 6

Preheat the oven to 180°C fan/200°C/400°F/Gas 6.

For the Chantilly Cream, put the cream, icing/confectioners' sugar and vanilla extract into a bowl and whisk with an electric hand-held whisk (or balloon whisk) until firm and silky, but be careful not to over whisk it. Cover and chill until ready to serve.

Prepare the pears by halving each one lengthways and use a paring knife to core and remove all the pips. Put them in a bowl and squeeze a little lemon juice over them to stop them oxidizing and turning brown.

Take a high-sided baking sheet big enough to hold all the pears in a single layer and pour in the wine, along with three-quarters of the sugar and stir until dissolved. Lay the pears cut-side-up in the baking sheet and drizzle the honey over the top of all of them. Follow this with the remaining sugar and dot a small knob/pat of the butter on each pear. Sprinkle the flaked/slivered almonds over the top and dust with cinnamon.

Nestle the geranium leaves amongst the pears and put in the preheated oven. Depending on the ripeness of your pears the cooking time may vary by 20 minutes, but on average they'll take just under 1½ hours. Check the pears halfway through cooking time and add a splash more wine if the liquid has reduced too much – this will form your syrup for serving so you want some left in there. The pears are done when they are soft if poked with a knife.

Serve with a dollop of the Chantilly Cream and the syrup drizzled over the top. You can serve the geranium leaves too as a pretty garnish if you want to.

GREEK WALNUT CAKE

Karidopita is an indulgent dessert cake. It is moist and unctuous, fabulous eaten freshly baked and even better a day or two later. Walnuts and warming spices are complemented by a heady Greek brandy-infused syrup that soaks into the fluffy sponge. I always use brown breadcrumbs to give it a deeper flavour whilst keeping it light in texture. Typical of many Mediterranean desserts, this is about sating that craving for something sweet at the end of a meal without eating a huge portion. Enjoy at your peril!

3 eggs
150 ml/⅔ cup light olive oil or vegetable oil
150 ml/⅔ cup whole milk
250 g/1¼ cups caster/granulated sugar
150 g/3 cups fresh brown breadcrumbs (see page 130)
150 g/1 cup semolina
200 g/2 scant cups coarse ground walnuts
1 tablespoon baking powder
1 tablespoon ground cinnamon
12 grates of nutmeg
¼ teaspoon ground cloves
walnut halves, to decorate

For the syrup
200 g/1 cup caster/superfine sugar
3 strips of orange zest, plus extra finely grated zest to garnish
2 cinnamon sticks
½ teaspoon vanilla extract
60 ml/¼ cup brandy (preferably Greek)

a baking pan/high-sided baking sheet (about 30 x 20 cm/ 12 x 8 inches), lightly oiled

Serves 12

Preheat the oven to 180°C fan/200°C/400°F/Gas 6.

First make the syrup. Combine all the ingredients in a heavy-based saucepan and add 200 ml/¾ cup cold water. Set over a medium heat, bring to a boil, then immediately turn off the heat and leave in the pan to cool.

To make the cake batter, put the eggs, oil, milk and sugar in a large bowl and beat together using a hand-held electric whisk. In a separate bowl mix together the breadcrumbs, semolina, ground walnuts, baking powder and spices. Slowly fold the dry mixture into the wet mixture until fully combined – use a spatula to do this.

Pour the cake batter into the oiled baking pan and bake in the preheated oven for 30 minutes, or until a knife inserted into the centre comes out clean. Leave to cool in the pan for 15 minutes.

Run a knife through the cake in portion sizes, either in diamond shapes as pictured or squares. Spoon the room-temperature syrup slowly over the warm cake (you can discard the orange zest and cinnamon). You'll think you've made too much syrup but you haven't, keep going until all the syrup is used, then leave the cake to rest for minimum 1 hour (although it tastes even better the next day!). Once done, garnish with the walnut halves and a sprinkle of orange zest. It's sticky so serve it with forks.

ROSE-SCENTED WHIPPED FROZEN YOGURT
WITH POMEGRANATE SYRUP

Whipped frozen yogurt fragranced with rosewater and drizzled with a sharp and sweet pomegranate syrup – here are all the headline ingredients of Cyprus in one refreshing mouthful. I use a Greek-style yogurt here, which is slightly thicker than natural yogurt but not set like traditional Greek yogurt.

350 g/1¼ cups Greek-style
   yogurt
80 g/scant ½ cup caster/
   superfine sugar
a pinch of salt
60 ml/¼ cup rosewater, or more
   to taste
about 2 tablespoons crushed
   pistachio kernels, to garnish

For the Pomegranate Syrup
2 fresh pomegranates (you will
   need about 220 g/1⅓ cups
   seeds), plus extra to garnish
75 g/heaping ⅓ cup caster/
   superfine sugar
a few drops of freshly squeezed
   lemon juice

a 500-ml/2-cup capacity lidded,
   freezerproof container

Serves 4

To remove the seeds from the pomegranates, fill a large bowl with cold water. Quarter each one, drop them into the water and use your hands to break away the seeds. They should sink to the bottom and the pith will float to the top. Skim off and discard the pith and scoop out the seeds, draining off any water.

Reserve a few tablespoons of the seeds to garnish and combine the rest with 125 ml/½ cup cold water, either in a bowl or the cup of a blender. Pulverize them in the bowl using a hand-held blender or blitz in the blender. Pass through a fine sieve/strainer into a small saucepan and stir in the sugar. Set the pan over a medium heat and simmer until the liquid has reduced by half or is thick enough to coat the back of a spoon. Add a few drops of lemon juice to the syrup and set aside to cool.

To make the whipped frozen yogurt, put the yogurt in a bowl and add the sugar, salt and rosewater and beat together to combine. The strength of a rosewater's flavour can vary by brand, so taste as you go, but remember freezing dulls flavour so I suggest you go for slightly stronger than you want it to taste once made at this stage.

Pour the yogurt mixture into a lidded freezerproof container and pop it into the freezer. After a few hours remove it from the freezer and whisk thoroughly with a fork to break up the ice crystals; if you can do this every few hours and repeat three times, great, but if not don't worry – as long as you get the first whisking in a few hours after it goes into the freezer it'll be fine.

Remove the frozen yogurt from the freezer for 15 minutes before you want to serve it to let it soften. Scoop into bowls and drizzle over a little of the pomegranate syrup. Garnish with the reserved pomegranate seeds and chopped pistachios.

CHAMOMILE GELATO
WITH WAFERS & FRESH HONEYCOMB

While Italian gelato and ice cream have similar base ingredients, gelato uses more milk than cream and is less whipped, so because there is less fat and air it has a more intense flavour. My chamomile-infused gelato has a delicate aroma and I serve it with pieces of honeycomb and wafers for a little crunch.

150 ml/⅔ cup double/heavy cream
625 ml/scant 2½ cups whole milk
100 g/½ cup caster/superfine sugar
½ teaspoon vanilla extract
2 tablespoons dried chamomile flowers (or the contents of 1 chamomile teabag)
1 tablespoon cornflour/cornstarch
1 tablespoon brandy (preferably Greek)
fresh honeycomb or runny honey, to serve

a high-sided metal baking pan, chilled in the fridge or freezer

a 1-litre/1-quart capacity lidded, freezerproof container

an ice cream machine (optional)

For the Wafers
160 g/scant 1¼ cups plain/all-purpose flour
80 g/heaping ⅓ cup caster/superfine sugar
1 teaspoon ground cinnamon
1 egg
1 tablespoon olive oil

2 baking sheets, 1 lined with baking parchment, plus an extra sheet of parchment

Serves 6

To make the gelato, put the cream, 500 ml/2 cups of the milk, the sugar, vanilla extract and chamomile in a large saucepan and set over a medium heat. Bring to the boil, stirring, then remove from the heat.

Mix the remaining milk with the cornflour/cornstarch in a small jug/pitcher to make a slurry. Once the cream and milk mixture has stopped bubbling, pour the slurry in while stirring continuously. Return the pan to a low heat and warm the mixture, stirring continuously, until it thickens and the very first bubbles start to appear on the surface, then remove from the heat and pour straight into the chilled baking pan. Let cool slightly then put in the fridge for about 2 hours.

Remove the mixture from the fridge and sieve/strain out the chamomile and discard. Stir in the brandy, pour it into a lidded freezerproof container and put it in the freezer for 2 hours, after which time either churn the mixture in your ice cream machine (following the manufacturers' instructions) or alternatively, leave it to freeze until almost solid then pulse in the cup of a blender in batches.

To make the wafers, preheat the oven to 180°C fan/200°C/400°F/Gas 6. Combine the flour, sugar and cinnamon in a mixing bowl. Add the egg, oil and 80 ml/⅓ cup cold water. Beat with an electric hand-held whisk until combined and thickened, then switch to a spatula and continue to mix until you have a thick sticky dough.

Fill a glass with water. Dip 2 teaspoons into the water and use these to spoon about 6 dots of dough onto the lined baking sheet, leaving plenty of space between them and dipping the spoons into the water each time. Lay a second sheet of baking parchment on top of the spooned dough and use the base of a pan to press down and create disks the thickness of a coin, about 10 cm/4 inches diameter. Lay a second baking sheet on top of the baking parchment. Bake like this in the preheated oven for 12–15 minutes. Remove the top baking sheet and peel the wafers off the parchment. Leave to cool and crisp up.

Serve the gelato in scoops, top with honeycomb and add wafers.

INDEX

ACKNOWLEDGEMENTS

Creating a cookbook is the result of dozens of people all working together in their respected disciplines, sharing one collective vision and transforming an idea into something tangible. I can never quite describe the sense of pride and satisfaction that I feel when I hear that 'thud', as the first copy of my new book falls through the letterbox. This book has my name on the front, but it's far from just my work. I'm always humbled and inspired by the people who help bring a project like *Rustica* to fruition as without any one of them, it would always remain just an idea.

At home, my family remains the bedrock of my life. My wife Anna who, as much as she denies it, I know enjoys endlessly tasting the same dish again and again and again (she doesn't) but thank you for putting up with me. My kids who have always been my harshest critics ('not dad's food again!' – ahhh, how I love hearing that!). I love you all.

My mum, dad and brothers, Stephan and Marcus – when I published my first book with Ryland Peters & Small, there were just a handful of us; and now we have multiplied in numbers and in joy with each new addition to the family. I always admire everything you guys do and owe a debt of gratitude I'll never be able to repay to my parents for a life of love and support. Except when I annoy you. There is also my extended family with too many names to mention, who I always count on for insight into a life that my generation won't truly appreciate – thank you for all those conversations and letting me plagiarize your recipes.

Cindy Richards, Publisher – without your belief in me none of this would have been possible, I am always proud and thoroughly enjoy working with you, thank you. Julia Charles, Editorial Director – you never cease to amaze me at how you can convert the scribblings of a madman into something not only legible but eloquent, thank you for that and for generally being brilliant. To the team who drive the vision of the book forward; Leslie Harrington, Art Director, and Sonya Nathoo, Designer – thank you both for humouring me and my thoughts on design ,and for creating something beautiful regardless... thanks to Kathy Kordalis, for recreating every recipe for the shoots and bringing your own flair (something I've always admired) to my recipes. Mowie Kay, where do I start? All the work culminates in your incredible images and as yet, you still refrain from admitting how much you photoshop pics of me – I'll always love you for that.

Finally, to all my friends and anyone else I haven't mentioned here who in some way helped shape what you are reading today – thank you.